Mary Porter Gamewell and The Siege of Peking

MARY PORTER GAMEWELL

Mary Porter Gamewell and The Siege of Peking

An American lady's experiences of the Boxer Uprising, China 1900

A. H. Tuttle

LEONAUR

Mary Porter Gamewell
and The Siege of Peking
An American lady's experiences of the
Boxer Uprising, China 1900
by A. H. Tuttle

First published under the titles
Mary Porter Gamewell
and Her Story
of the Siege of Peking

Leonaur is an imprint
of Oakpast Ltd

Copyright in this form © 2010 Oakpast Ltd

ISBN: 978-0-85706-138-6 (hardcover)
ISBN: 978-0-85706-137-9 (softcover)

http://www.leonaur.com

Publisher's Notes

In the interests of authenticity, the spellings, grammar and place names
used have been retained from the original editions.

The opinions of the authors represent a view of events in which she
was a participant related from her own perspective,
as such the text is relevant as an historical document.

The views expressed in this book are not necessarily
those of the publisher.

Contents

Preface

Mary Porter Gamewell's missionary career (1871-1906) covers the heroic age of the Woman's Foreign Missionary Society of the Methodist Episcopal Church in China. She was one of the first missionaries whom the Society sent to that country. Her marriage eleven years later did not in any measure interrupt her work, for having no children, she continued full service, broken only by an occasional visit to her native land. And during these home visits, which were supposed to be periods of rest, she was tireless in the use of her tongue and pen for the great cause to which she had consecrated her life. In 1906 her name was enrolled on the scroll of the immortals "who were slain for the Word of God, and for the testimony which they held."

It was during the last years of her life that those great events occurred that culminated in the astonishing revolution in the attitude of the imperial government of China toward modern scholarship and Christian civilization, and which was the beginning of a new era in missionary work in that country, which until then presented a stubborn and murderous resistance to the gospel.

We owe it to the memory of the heroines, who, amid great perils and immeasurable sacrifices, pioneered the frontiers of heathendom, to record the story while it is fresh in our memories. And we owe it to the church of the future to furnish it with the answers to the questions which a Christianized China is sure to ask: "Who wrought this miracle, and by what means was it done?" We should do what we can to perpetuate the inspiration of those early days into all subsequent ages. The best way to do this is not to wait for some future historian to tabulate the general facts, and study their causes and relations. Philosophical history is not half so vital nor truthful as the personal story of individual actors in that history. As Aristotle has said, "a thing is more than the sum of all its parts." There must be added what he calls the "*ousia*," its innermost reality, its essence, which makes this sum a thing. So the best way to know events is to know the individuals who lived in them and made them.

Even doctrines are best understood in that way. The best way to know Christianity is to know Christ and the apostles. To feel the pulse of the church's life, we must touch human hearts, hear their moans and their songs, become familiar with their daily thoughts, and walk with them along the homely pathway of duty—things too common-place to demand a page in formal history, and yet things that make the very *ousia* of life.

For this reason, we have consented to collate the material which Mrs. Gamewell has left, and as nearly as possible construct an auto-biographical sketch of one woman whose life is fairly representative of many others who prepared the way of the coming of the Lord in China. There have been loaned us for this purpose journals, personal letters, and many articles prepared by her for the press. Among this material are two things of great historic value, which have not been seen, even by her intimate friends. One is a journal of the Chungking riot of 1886, which was written while she was a prisoner in the *yamen* of the magistrate during that tragic event.

This journal was fortunately preserved uninjured by the Boxers who destroyed our Mission property in Peking in 1900. The second thing is her own story of the siege in Peking, prepared by her for the press, from copious notes which she had made during the siege. Fully three fourths of this volume is from her pen. She was herself a gifted writer, having a literary quality in her style, which makes the facts she records quiver with life. And the facts themselves are rich in colour, varied incident, and wide meanings. Here we have poetry, romance, tragedy, and religion; and amid it all we discern the presence of Him who rules the centuries, doing the work of eternity in guiding one of his trusting children day by day, along ways and by deeds of which the world takes no heed, but which resistlessly are bringing his kingdom to earth.

CHAPTER 1

A Missionary in Preparation

Mary Q. Porter, who one day was to become Mrs. Frank D. Gamewell, was the second child in a family of three daughters and two sons. Her parents were born in England, but she came to them in Allegheny City, Pennsylvania, on the twentieth day of October, 1848, some years after they had made the United States their home.

Every positive personality, such as hers, has its spring, like the River Jordan, in some Hermon, which pours out its crystal streams in the fountains of Dan and Banias. Its character is modified by its tributaries and the country through which it passes, but its elemental capacities, which are ever present, are best studied at its sources. Her father, Nathaniel Porter, came of an old English family in Stratford-on-Avon; and the name frequently appears in the annals of that town back to the days of Shakespeare. The father of Nathaniel was a man of strong religious character and a master of a college preparatory school in his native town; and his son received a most careful intellectual as well as religious training.

After he came of age he was given a generous sum of money and came to America, where he met Miss Maria Killingley, who had come here with her widowed father in 1833. They were married at Allegheny City, Pennsylvania, in 1845, and fifteen years later settled in Davenport, Iowa, which was their home for many years. Mr. Porter was a gentleman by birth and by culture. He had a mind alert and acute, was an exceptionally gifted conversationalist, and was widely informed on all the great subjects that were agitating the minds of men. Had nature added to his other native qualities the genius for affairs, his daughter's career probably would have been very different from that which is here recorded.

Mrs. Porter was the daughter of Henry Killingley and Maria Whittaker. She was born near Nottingham, England, and remembered how, when a little girl, she "often gathered daisies in the shadow of Nottingham Castle." Her mother died when she was an infant, and her father brought her to the United States, intending to make this country his home. But his heart drew him back to where the wife of his youth lay buried. His daughter, however, had no longing for the land of her early sorrow, and she decided to remain where she could make her own career unhampered by ancient family traditions. She, however, had been well born, and her past, far more than she knew, was a force which carried her to her destiny. She came of a people of sterling worth, in whom conscience was the law of life, and who placed duty infinitely above gain.

She was one who would not weakly succumb to difficulties but would bravely meet and, if possible, master them.

During her residence in Allegheny City she became intensely interested in the study of a case of illness in her family; and with the generous approval of Mr. Porter, hired a housekeeper to care for her home while she pursued a course of study in the Woman's Medical College in Philadelphia, from which she graduated with honour in 1859. Afterward she studied Homeopathy and began the practice of medicine in that school, making Davenport, Iowa, her home. It was a brave thing for a woman in those days to enter a profession which heretofore had been monopolized by men, and which was popularly supposed would detract from the charm of femininity of character. But she triumphed, demonstrating in her own person what is now everywhere accepted, that every noble calling is consistent with every womanly quality.

Mrs. Porter was one of the foremost women of Iowa in the organization of women for the relief of suffering during the Civil War and the troublous times immediately subsequent. She was intimately associated with Mrs. Wittenmeyer in the organisation of the Soldiers' Orphans' Home of Iowa, which is now located at Davenport. Thus Mary was born and bred in an atmosphere of intellectuality and conscientious endeavour. She grew up in the conviction that a woman's horizon was not to be bounded by the four walls of her home: that worldwide views really sweetened and enriched the home life. We have not been able to gather many incidents with which to construct the story of her childhood. There are no traditions of any singular precocity, prematurely revealing her exceptional career. The aureole of the martyr spirit was not suggested in the rosy-faced, happy child of those early years. In all her correspondence, we have found but a single allusion to it, and it was written May 10, 1906, a few months before her translation:

I am going down town to take a snapshot of the old Fifth Street house. It is an old ramshackle now, in a street taken up by the railroad. It used to stand in the shadow of great trees and in a street filled with homes of Davenport's best people. And though the railroad was there, open green and Court House Square, full of trees and covered with grass, met the eye over the single track. You know that the elevated way fills much of the street now and cuts off the green expanse on the south.

I started for China from that house. On the floor of that house I sat out the night in miserable wonder over a hurt delivered by one I had revered, and *held on* when my inexperience could not *see* how He was justified.

That holding on saved the day for me and brought results which shall abide until I see Him and am satisfied. How plainly the way appears when we look on it from the heights to which it led! How one quivers to see the turning points and crossroads at which it would have been *so easy* to have lost the way! There God's constraining power held, and we only just let him, so bewildered and occupied within our limited horizon that we could not see that he was doing anything at all!

"I ran to that house the day we heard at school that southern guns had fired on Fort Sumter. From there I went into the excited and illuminated street the night that the country rejoiced over the fall of Vicksburg, and from the windows of that house I looked with sinking heart at flags flying at half-mast because Lincoln was dead—dead by an assassin's hand.

Yes, the days spent in that old house were, for me, full of growing pains.

Her occasional reference in conversation to that period of her life was more like the fragrance of the marigold, heavily laden with the spirit of the past rather than with definite memories. The secret of her almost unbroken silence concerning those years was probably the fact that the child had a premonition that the future was to bring her into a life in which she would hold a place of conspicuous and far-reaching usefulness. The thoughtful girl was ever on the lookout, inquiring what might be the work to which she was destined. She was living more in the things to come than in the immediate present. Not that her childhood was unhappy, for it was sweet with innocence, culture, and love; but to her outreaching mind it was the enchanted stream bearing her ever down the years to where the castle of her dreams stood, all glorious.

A companion of those early days writes of her and another schoolmate, who with herself made a trio of intimate friendships in work and play, which continued on into mature years. She says: "Mattie and I recognized that she and I were kindred spirits, and that Mary was one with us, but with a difference. She loved fun and frolic as well as did we, and could play a full part; but we felt that at the same time, with all her love for sport, there was something more: a gentle seriousness and earnestness of purpose that were a restraining influence whenever our lighter spirits might seem to carry us beyond the bounds of innocent mirth or strict propriety. But any rebuke from her would come in the guise of gentle effort to turn our thoughts toward something safer and better. She was fond of singing, and often the diversion would be a call to the piano; and the singing of hymns would close the enjoyment of a happy evening spent in one or another of our homes." One of these two companions of Mary testified to her recognition of the more earnest and religious elements of her character by impulsively asking her mother: "Why is it that Mary is always good and I am sometimes bad?"

"After their dear schoolmate had confessed Christ and united with the church these two young comrades noted that the desire that they too should share with her the joy she had found was manifest in many loving ways in all their intercourse together, while in other things she was still the same bright, merry, fun-loving companion as before." She occasionally told of how, when a very little girl, her imagination transformed the chairs in her room into benighted heathen, and how she became a missionary, destroying their idols and bringing to them the light of the gospel. But she did not tell that which we are curious to know: what awakened this spirit in her heart. It is doubtful whether she herself remembered what it was; and it is almost certain that the unknown sower of the precious seed never knew what he had done. What a surprise it will be to him when the sheaves are gathered!

We have the testimony of her own lips that in those days she was peculiarly sensitive to the sights and sounds of Nature. One Sunday morning in the summer of 1902, while outing on the coast of Maine, we took a walk together two miles or more inland to attend service in the Methodist church in the nearest village. On our return, in order to protect ourselves from the heat of the noonday sun, we made a detour from the main road through a dense forest, in the deep silence of which we could hear voices which could not be heard under the open sky. Mrs. Gamewell asked me if I could understand what God was saying in this old cathedral of nature. I replied: "I hear the voices; please articulate them for me." She began with, "All nature is an interpreter of the spiritual realm," and continued to talk till every leaf and stone, every speck of sunshine and every shadow seemed vocal-spoken words of God. When we passed out into the open sunshine I asked her when she first became conscious of this identity of Nature and the eternal Word; and she answered, "From my childhood."

This faculty, then, was in her a gift rather than the result of culture. Its basis was an original temperament, closely allied to that of a poet, a delicate sensibility of organization which makes the human heart a living Æolian harp, catching and rendering every rustle of Nature.

There were two things that occurred in those years that powerfully affected her character and determined her career: the Civil War and her conversion. She was but thirteen years of age when the scream of Bellona terrified the country. And during the most impressible period of a girl's life, when the observant soul is inquiring for the meaning of things occurring within and without, the entire land was absorbed in the tremendous conflict raging between the North and the South. She saw regiments of Iowans, in which were many of her personal friends, marching away to the music of fife and drum for the field of carnage. She heard the sobs of many mothers and wives who had given their dear ones, an immeasurable sacrifice for their country's honour.

She was still a girl when the war closed; and she saw battle-worn veterans returning home, with their ranks decimated, and in many instances almost annihilated. But she was old enough to understand that this was the price paid for two things: the nation's unity, and the freedom of all its citizens; and it was borne in upon her that this sacrifice was none too great for so glorious a consummation.

In those days the natural instinct of patriotism was intensified until it became with her a passion. A feature of that passion was its breadth. While she dearly loved her home city and her state, her love widened out, its heat increasing with the volume of its flame, till it enwrapped the whole land. So charged was her heart with this holy passion, that when she rose, as we have frequently seen her, and stretching out her hand, ejaculated, "My country!" it sent an electric thrill to all who heard her.

It was during the war, when she was but fifteen years of age, that she publicly consecrated her life to God, and was received in the Methodist Episcopal Church in Davenport, Iowa. There was nothing phenomenal or spectacular in that experience. She often spoke of far more apparent changes in the unfolding of her divine life, when she passed crises in later years, than that that occurred when she first confessed Christ. The probability is that she was an accepted child of God before that time, living a life of prayer and childlike innocence. Her so-called conversion was but little more than an open confession—a stage in the normal development of her spiritual character. It was perfectly natural that the sentiments awakened in her heart by the great national conflict should impress themselves on her understanding of her spiritual life.

Whether or not she was aware of the process at the time, the fact was shaping itself in her mind, of which she afterward became fully conscious, that God's kingdom was wider than the bounds of any church or country, that everywhere men should be brought into the liberty of this kingdom, and finally, that the soldiers of Christ should hesitate at no sacrifice to secure this end. Thus the missionary thought lay like the seed of God's truth in her heart. It was a potent factor in her spirit long before she discovered its bearing on her lifework, for which God was preparing her. Mary Porter studied in the public schools in the several cities where she had lived during her childhood, and was in the High School of Davenport, Iowa, when the Orphans' Home was transferred to that city.

When she was nearly eighteen years of age she left the school to take a position of teacher in the Home. After teaching for one year, she returned to the High School, and by her indomitable industry not only graduated with the class from which she had been absent a full year, but took such high rank and so impressed the principal, who had been elected head of the Grandview Academy, Grandview, Iowa, that he offered her the position of teacher of Latin, physiology and English grammar in that school. In a letter written many years later she speaks of that year of doubled toil thus:

I used to pray for such help when crowded to desperation in my last year's work before graduation. I felt justified in crowding under the circumstances, and I had a right to expect God to bless my efforts, and he did. I used to ask him to help me with geometry, Latin, chemistry, and everything in which I was likely to stagger from overwork. I have sat down to my desk so weary and discouraged with everything that I could have almost cried; but in the extremity I would remember God, and have felt his unmistakable help; and so the puzzles disappeared and I wondered where I found them. Now, in those days I could not have told my faith, words would have stuck in my throat; indeed, I was in great measure unconscious of the faith I exerted. In my extremity I called upon him for things I had not heard men say we might expect from God, and God himself taught me to come again and again until my faith strengthened, and I naturally looked to him without being driven to it.

After graduation, in 1868, she accepted the position offered her in the Grandview Academy, and taught there for more than two years, continuing her studies preparatory for a regular college course. Though but twenty years of age, she was made superintendent of the Sunday school and did much religious work among the students. While there her thought was turned to the foreign missionary work; and at the close of the year she resigned her position in the Academy and accepted a call from the Woman's Foreign Missionary Society to devote her life to the cause of Christ in China.

After leaving Grandview she taught several months in Davenport schools, during which time she made her final arrangements to go to China, and left her home for that purpose October 9, 1871. Hearing that there was another Mary Porter in the city of Peking, to which she was destined, she decided, in order to avoid confusion, to place a middle letter in her name. What shall it be? Q is the initial letter of *Quo*, what? Let it be Q. Henceforth till her marriage her name stands Mary Q. Porter.

CHAPTER 2

From America to Peking

Mrs. Gamewell had purposed to publish a *History of the Peking Station of North China Mission of The Woman's Foreign Missionary Society of the Methodist Episcopal Church*, and had prepared copious notes from which we extract the following:

The North China Mission of the Methodist Episcopal Church was organized the same year that gave birth to the Woman's Foreign Missionary Society (1869). In October of that year, while Bishop Kingsley was present, the Mission passed a resolution asking the bishop to appoint two single women to organize a girls' boarding school and to conduct evangelistic work among women. This request was sent to the Woman's Foreign Missionary Society. The executive committee at its meeting in May, 1871, authorized the New England Branch to send to Peking Miss Maria Brown, of Melrose, Massachusetts, and the Western Branch to send Miss Mary Porter, of Davenport, Iowa. They were accordingly appointed and instructed to go to work under the direction of the married women of the mission, Mrs. L. N. Wheeler and Mrs. H. H. Lowry.

At the same meeting of the executive committee Miss Beulah Woolston and Miss Sarah Woolston, who, under the direction of the Parent Board, had been doing missionary work in Foochow since 1859, and were now taking a well-earned rest at home in the United States, were adopted by the Woman's Foreign Missionary Society, and were instructed to continue their work in Foochow in its name and under its support.

In 1871 these four women tried to make a party across the continent to San Francisco, but the Chicago fire was raging and interrupted communication, so that they were not able to make connection till Miss Porter met the others in San Francisco. In those days nothing was known by the missionary authorities in the United States about the closing of navigation during the winter between Shanghai and Tientsin. As the Misses Brown and Porter had started too late to reach North China that autumn, they went south with the Misses Woolston and spent the winter in Foochow.

The following is taken from a letter of personal reminiscences written several years later:

Close on to Christmas of 1871 we two—that is, Maria Brown and I—sat in a room in Foochow, China. The ceiling was high and the wide, long floor was painted in stripes. A wood fire burned in the grate and a big door opened into a bathroom. When I wanted to be alone, I went into the bathroom and put my head out of the window into the unoccupied space of the upper air. One day, with my head out of the window, I struggled alone with a load of responsibility with which, in my youthful, opinionated state and crudity of spiritual development, I scorned to trouble God.

Suddenly without request or thought of mine, my heart went free and a specific conviction concerning the matters that troubled me seemed to flood my being with knowledge as sure as if a voice had spoken from Heaven. Thereafter no thought of those matters could cause fear or trouble of any kind. Years afterward everything turned out exactly as I was made to know that day, and was confident through all following days, they would. The experience was a sacred wonder hid in my heart, and was the beginning of a series of new and uplifting lessons concerning God's care and love, by which he made me more fit for the work which I was to do.

The experience stands in vivid relief among the Providences that attended the development of the school. "Miss Brown and I had been sent out to open a school for girls in Peking. What, then, were we doing away down south in Foochow? At the time of our outgoing the Woman's Foreign Missionary Society was only two years old, and the women of that Society did not know as much as they do now. They did not know that the approach to Tientsin, the port of Peking, freezes, and that vessels do not run north from Shanghai after freezing weather sets in. So they sent us out, to land in Shanghai after the last vessel going north had departed. But we were travelling with Miss Beulah and Miss Sarah Woolston. They were pioneer workers among Chinese women and girls twelve years before there was a Woman's Foreign Missionary Society. They had established a school for girls in Foochow and done a wide-reaching work through the church there that endeared them to all hearts.

The Misses Woolston, their work and themselves being adopted by the newly organized Woman's Foreign Missionary Society, were now returning to China from a well-earned vacation. They took us with them to Foochow, to wait there for the opening of navigation, in the spring. Thus the same Providence which had given us raw recruits the high privilege of going to meet the new life in the new field in the companionship of such veterans as the devoted and talented Misses Woolston gave us also all the advantages of a winter spent in an old mission, where we could learn lessons from such successful and established work as that developed by Miss Beulah and Miss Sarah Woolston.

Though one day, when it was told us that one of the pupils had rolled downstairs and knocked out a tooth in her progress, and that Miss Sarah had picked up the child and the tooth, put the latter into its place, and bandaged the child's mouth shut until the tooth had grown fast again, we wondered if we should ever be equal to the exigencies of school work in China.

While in Foochow the two young women studied the characters and principles of the Chinese language, but made no effort to acquire the pronunciation of the South which differed so radically from that of the North where they were to labour. As soon as navigation opened they started for Peking, where they arrived April 6, 1872. We have no account of the trip written at the time; but in 1905 Mrs. Gamewell published an article in The Chautauquan, in which she describes the journey in part as seen in the perspective of thirty-three years:

Our course lies northward from Shanghai over troubled seas till we pass between the rocky promontory of Shantung and the point of Port Arthur. The Gulf of Pechili about the promontory of Shantung is one of the roughest bits of water to be found, and its choppy sea will usually bring to grief the best of sailors. Sailing across the gulf, our steamer anchors outside the bar which bars the entrance to the mouth of the muddy and exceedingly winding river Pei Ho (North River). During neap tide a steady wind will blow the water off the bar until there is not enough left to float even so small a vessel as the little coast steamship, so that our vessel must anchor outside and leave us tossing on the short waves of the stormy Gulf, waiting for less wind and more water, in misery remembering sympathetically the man who was so seasick that he feared he should die, and later on was afraid that he would not.

The captains of these coastwise steamers are a picturesque set— soldiers of fortune, with vocabularies gathered from all parts of the world; and with full steam ahead and with bubbling vocabularies the vessel goes grinding over, while the sound of scraping and grinding during the passage testifies to the fact that it has not only ploughed the waves, but also the sands below.

The coast line near the mouth of the Pei Ho presents only a long stretch of mud flats. In the village of Ta Ku, on the flats, live the pilots who own and navigate a great fleet of steam tugs which serve over the bar and up the river.

There is a hotel at Ta Ku, and during the summer months the people from Tientsin frequently resort there for the sea air, but in recent years the greater part of the foreign population seek Pei Tai Ho, which lies eastward near Shan Hai Kuan, and is becoming known as the Newport of China. Commanding the entrance to the river are the Ta Ku forts, which repulsed the British and French fleets in 1859, but were taken the following year by a rear attack. They now lie in ruin, battered and dismantled. Having crossed the bar the little vessel steams around the many bends by which the Pei Ho makes its way to the sea, frequently running aground and making some of the curves by deliberately pushing her nose into the mud bank and being pulled around by cables.

Though Tientsin lies but thirty miles inland from the sea, it is usually a day's trip by the crooked, winding river, so that most passengers now leave the steamer at the mouth of the river and hurry on to Tientsin by the train which runs along its banks. Tientsin lies on the west bank of the Pei Ho at a point below the junction of the river with the Grand Canal. The old city with its suburbs stretches along the river for six miles or more and up the canal an equal distance, and contains a population of over a million, though if the census were to include all those living in the houseboats swarming the river and canal for miles, the population would probably be found to be twice this number.

If you wish to reach Peking, you may now hurry on by train, but if you wish to see China, there are two ways of making the trip. One is by native houseboat to Tung Chou, which is at the head of navigation, then from Tung Chou by sedan chair, or cart, or donkey. The other mode of travel is by cart. A gentleman very soberly told us that he knew a man who left Tientsin in a cart, and with the first propelling jerk of the mules, he left his seat on the bottom of the cart and never landed there again until the cart drew up outside the walls of Peking, having been shaken about in his cart all day like a peppercorn in a continuously shaken pepper box.

We chose the river and the houseboat. The skies were clear, the winds in our favour, and the men who were to pole, scull, and sail our little boat were in high good humour. They shoved off with shoutings that mingled with the shouts of hundreds of other boatmen, many of whom, with poles armed with spikes and hooks, helped our boatmen pull and push away through a jam of boats that throng the river all the way from the settlement to the native city of Tientsin and beyond. As we approached the Pontoon Bridge, or Bridge of Boats, as it is often called, a clumsy barge slowly dropped from its place in a line of barges that formed the bridge.

Our boat was only one of many which waited their turn to pass through the gap thus made in the bridge. A crowd of foot passengers and burden-bearers were waiting on the edge of this break in this bridge; but they did not seem to mind the delay, so absorbed were they in the contemplation of the foreigners, who seemed to afford them quite as much amusement as a bear performance or a monkey show.

Above the bridge we passed other bridges, and were at last out of the throng of boats and well on our way up the winding Pei Ho. As our boat swung around the various curves we were often in sight of the ruined Catholic cathedral which occupies a prominent site on the banks of the river. This cathedral was burned at the time of the Tientsin massacre in 1870. After being restored it was again destroyed in 1900.

The country between Tientsin and Tung Chou is flat and unin-
teresting, but in the time of standing grain and full foliage, with
clear skies and a fair breeze, the passage up the Pei Ho is very
enjoyable. The wind filled our bamboo-slatted sail, a competent
and good-natured captain held the rudder, and with the sliding
panels that formed the sides of our boat taken out we reclined
at our ease and listened to the purling waters and watched the
green banks not far away on either side. We tied to the bank
at night and sailed away in the early gray of the succeeding
mornings.

The bottom of this river in many places lies higher than the
surrounding country, and sometimes during the floods the water breaks through the banks and spreads many miles through
the low-lying fields. At such times boats instead of following
the course of the river around its many curves, sail in a straight
course. I have had such boat trips in which we passed over the
tops of fields of *kaoliang*, a kind of broom corn, which stood
at least ten feet high, and the villages built on land somewhat
higher than the surrounding fields appeared as islands in the
surrounding water.

At Tung Chou, twelve miles from the east gate of Peking, all
boats land their passengers and unload their freight, which are
transported in carts or wheelbarrows, or on mules or donkeys.
Eight *li* from Tung Chou (a *li* is a third of a mile) the way to
Peking leads over a famous bridge which is called the Eight Li
Bridge. When the English and French marched against Peking
in 1860 it was the scene of one of the fiercest fights.

The Rev. L. N. Wheeler and his little daughter had met Miss Porter
and her companion, Miss Brown, at Tientsin, and had accompanied
them up the river. From Tung Chou they rode on donkeys, a mode
of conveyance so new to Miss Porter that she found it impossible to
retain her seat, and was frequently cast to the ground. They, however,
regarded these mishaps as interesting events which gave colour to an
otherwise dull picture. The landscape about the city is monotonous in
the extreme. The sombre gray walls rise fifty feet above the plain, and
over the city hangs a great cloud of dust. The picture was certainly not
one calculated to relieve the ache of homesickness which oppressed
the heart of a young woman whose kin were on the other side of the
globe.

The ridiculous donkey ride probably relieved that dreadful mental strain which he alone knows who looks in the dusk of the evening upon a great crowd of foreigners who hate him and his God, and who away from all his relatives goes through the gates of a heathen city which henceforth he is to call "my home." At the gates the party took Peking carts to convey them in greater privacy through the narrow and treeless streets with great walls shutting from view the private residences and their surrounding gardens. At last, after almost half a year since she bade *adieu* to her country and loved ones, she stood at the door of the Methodist Mission compound on Filial Piety Lane.

CHAPTER 3

The Gospel in China

Miss Porter entered Peking sixty-five years after Robert Morrison, the first Protestant apostle to China, had begun his lonely work in Canton. He, however, had been hampered by governmental restrictions and that temperamental conservatism which had preserved this great people practically unchanged through millenniums from away beyond the origin of Christianity or, possibly, that of the Jewish nation. It was seven years before he baptized the first native convert, and one year after his death (1834) there were but two Protestant missionaries in the empire, and the Christian Church had but three native members. Two things were required to prepare the way for the kingdom of God in that land. There must first occur certain providential events to break down the external restrictions to the gospel; and then the evangelists must find a way to let the gospel light into the minds of a people who, so far from desiring it, sincerely believed it to be a devilish wickedness, the secret of their national shame and disaster.

The history of the propaganda of the faith elsewhere would lead us to look for great world-movements, in which there was no conscious purpose to spread the gospel, but which would inerrantly serve that end. Egypt, Assyria, Babylon, Persia, Macedonia, and Rome were the unconscious servants of the Almighty in the ancient days. So in modern times, nations with purposes of conquest and greed have been unwittingly the avenging sword of the Lord.

It was England that became the providential instrument of opening the door for the entrance of the gospel in China. In attempting to protect the interests of commerce, after the retirement of the East India Company from China, England became involved in what is known as the opium war, which ended in 1842 in the Treaty of Nanking, which opened five ports for free foreign trade, and incidentally threw wide open the gates for the missionary. War broke out again, in which the Chinese government was humbled by British prowess, and another treaty was ratified in 1860 which granted the representatives of foreign governments the privilege of residence in the capital city, Peking, gave them passports to travel in all parts of China, and a guarantee that they should have protection in their religion.

Thus the way was prepared for the missionary to carry his message to the very doors of the imperial palace. The Presbyterian and the American Boards of Foreign Missions hastened at once to enter the city. Romanism had already been there for centuries. But it was not till 1869 that the Methodist Episcopal Church sent its representatives to that strategic centre. It was during that year that the Rev. L. N. Wheeler and the Rev. H. H. Lowry went up from Foochow "to spy out the land," and, like Caleb and Joshua, reported, "It is a goodly land, and we are well able to possess it." They at once went to work with zeal to lay the foundations of what has since become one of our most conspicuous and successful missions. The New Connection brethren at Tientsin very generously loaned them for six months one of their most efficient native preachers. And they were in sympathetic touch with the other Protestant missions in the city.

The prohibitive barriers which the national government had opposed to the presence and work of missionaries were broken by the force of war. It now remained for these missionaries to find a way by which to let the gospel light into the hearts of the people. The problem was not as simple as those familiar with the evangelism of the Western nations would suppose. The conditions were altogether different from those which the apostles encountered when they went out under the command, "*Go ye into all the world, and preach the gospel to every creature.*" The Greek mind, which for centuries had dominated the thought of the world, was alert, curious, ready to examine every new thing.

The Roman mind was as cosmopolite as it was imperial, believing that within every widely prevailing faith there was an element of truth; tolerant, even when perplexed with conflicting doctrines; asking earnestly, though sometimes despairingly, "What is truth?" The Jewish people scattered throughout the world had made the thoughtful mind familiar with those great principles which opened their perfect bloom in Christ; and this ubiquitous people furnished a starting place for the evangelists. In addition to that, the Western world was exhausted. It had outgrown its ancient thought.

Every modern science was but a weak modification of an older and better one; every song like the Æneid, was an imitation of an older and nobler one like the Iliad; every pleasure was an old one exaggerated. Modern religion had become an artificial performance void of all vitality. The Western world was consciously dying, longing for a fresh breath from the creative source of life to rejuvenate it and send it on a higher career of endeavour. To that dying world the gospel was literally the breath of life, which saved it not only spiritually but politically and in every other way.

The conditions in the Eastern world were totally different. We are not yet certain whence came the Chinese. If they are not indeed the ancient Sumerians, who appear on the remotest frontiers of human history, having already attained a high civilization at Babylon, four millenniums before Christ, it is certain that the civilizations of these people are identical. They are the same in their industry, their literary character, their instinctive abhorrence of brutal war, with its military aristocracy, and their principles of government.

It is also certain that they emigrated from that cradle of the human race. While the historic races with which we are familiar moved westward, following "the star of empire," this people moved eastward till they were stopped by the billows of the Pacific. Unaffected by the great events which prepared the Western world for the gospel of the kingdom, they built up a civilization entirely their own, developing a literature, science, and art, which antedated by centuries those of the European world. They had their vices, their rebellions, their frequent changes of dynasties, yet through it all the government moved on in its ancient way, and the normal development of the people was undisturbed.

They have had a history long enough to enable them to fathom the deeps of every religious system that had ever reached them, and to properly estimate its value. The mysticism of Buddhism had failed. Its temples are neglected. So far as it relates to the religious life of the people, that imported faith of India is only a broken shell of a nut, the meat of which was decayed. The atheistic faith of Taoism had practically ceased to be a computable force in the land; an intellectual system as lifeless as Patristic scholasticism is with us. The moral system of Confucius, beautiful as it is, has proved itself in the long test of the years to be utterly inadequate "to make the comers thereunto perfect." The ethics of the ages are a spent force. There is no hierarchy to deceive the people with a form of religion in the place of its reality, for the emperor is himself the representative of heaven and earth and the people, and relegates none of his glory to another. But the recent wars of China with foreign nations have shaken the faith of the people in the divinity of their rulers.

Amid all these changes, there is one thing in the faith of China which stands unmoved and apparently immovable: the people adore the Past. The holy thing is that which *has* been, coming down to them from the dawn of time. They fear and abhor change. The worship of ancestors is the soul of their religion. If this invulnerable conservatism which so appals the preacher of Christ were the torpor of a stagnant mind or the decrepitude of old age, it would not be so hopeless. But while China outages all other living nations the individual Chinaman has all the virile traits of youth. He is described by such as have laboured with him for many years as "an emigrant of ubiquitous adaptation; a business man, a mechanic, a trader, a sailor, a diplomat." He has not been a soldier, for he has too lofty a conception of the meaning of a man, to honour him whose chief business in life is just to fight and butcher his fellow. He explained China's disastrous war with Japan thus: "We are literary; they are only fighters."

We in these latter days have discovered that aid China is, after all, a youthful Hercules who even now is squeezing the serpents in his cradle. But when Miss Porter entered Peking these latent forces were not so apparent. It was her business, with her *colaborers*, to believe that these forces were there, find them out, awaken them by the gospel power of life, and at last, when God's hour should strike, send them forth not a horde of barbarians to threaten Christendom, but a redeemed host carrying the banner of peace. How our missionaries did this miracle, and by what means, it is the purpose of these sketches to tell.

CHAPTER 4

Home in Peking

The two apostles of Methodism in North China, the Rev. L. N. Wheeler and the Rev. H. H. Lowry, were reinforced in the fall of 1870 by the arrival of the Rev. L. W. Pilcher, of blessed memory, and the Rev. G. R. Davis, who, with the skill of a veteran, is still doing efficient service in this field. Their work, however, was necessarily preliminary—studying the situation, mastering the language, erecting chapels and other buildings, and pioneering the outlying country. The official reports of our brethren to the Mission Board during those first three years of the North China Mission, are both pathetic and inspiring. From the world view-point the situation was as hopeless as was the evangelization of Europe when Paul and Silas landed in Macedonia. But these four men faced the despairing conditions with a courage and faith worthy the inspired missionaries.

A property covering a little less than two acres, inclosed in a high brick wall, and lying not far from the city gates, was purchased. It had been formerly occupied by a chancellor of the empire as a place of residence for his family of twenty-seven wives and a large retinue of servants. Many of the buildings in this compound had to be torn down, and others erected and adapted to missionary purposes. This work, however, because of financial considerations, could not be done at once, and the missionaries were compelled to adjust themselves to their limitations, living in old Chinese houses adapted as nearly as possible to American habits of life. The appropriation for the entire work that year was less than $7,000. Into this environment came the first representatives of the Woman's Foreign Missionary Society, Miss Maria Brown and Miss Mary Q. Porter.

In a booklet entitled *Our Peking School*, which she published some sixteen years later, she gives us a delicious reminiscence which is better than a photograph of her Peking home, for it reproduces the glow of the atmosphere of her first day there, and gives us charming glimpses into her own heart as she stands upon the threshold of a work for which she was destined to lay down her life:

'You must be vaccinated!' The doctor was called! The deed was done! And Miss Brown and I, having just landed in Tientsin, *en route* to Peking, tarried there and nursed our wounded arms; and were, by so much, better prepared to meet the ills of the flesh, which, as well as the enemy of souls, should confront us in days to come.

First among memories of those first days, naturally enough, stands one of this experience which met us on the threshold of the new life to which we had come, and other memories throng in rapid succession. They are so vivid, that one cannot think how unreal they may seem to those who read these pages.

It was a hot April day in China—hot enough for a July day in America. We had come by boat from Tientsin to Tung Chou, and were on the road that lies between Tung Chou and Peking. It is a stone-paved road, and the huge paving stones are worn into deep ruts by the heavy wheelbarrows and carts that for ages have wheeled back and forth between the two cities.

There were five of us, and we were riding on donkeys—the superintendent of our North China Mission and his little daughter, a brother missionary, Miss Brown, and myself. Our saddles were stuffed packs, which long use had packed into anything but comfortable shape. On our several packs, three of our party balanced with no support for the feet, as the stirrups were hung over the packs on ropes, in a way that made it necessary to ride astride, in order to make any use of them.

Chinese women, when they ride, either sit astride or cross their feet in front, sitting tailor fashion on broad packs. This latter is the more easily done, since a driver runs after each animal and lends a steadying hand over rough places. The fashion in riding in China differing from the fashion of the West, there were no side-saddles for our use, so we undertook, as best we could, to adapt the fashion of the West to the saddle of the East. In my case this was all the more difficult, because the animal which I rode had an evil propensity for leaping the inequalities of the road. He volunteered many jumps into the air, which brought

28

me with as many involuntary jumps to the ground.

'My saddle is just like a hill,' complained the child riding ahead of me. An exclamation from behind called attention to another uncomfortable rider, who sat upon a donkey that was kicking out vigorously, just as the driver threw himself over the flying heels and with his arms around the animal's body strove to hold him to the ground. Presently there was a vision of our escort, with full-spread umbrella, sailing over the head of the donkey upon which he had been sitting, while for the instant that animal stood head down and heels in the air. Submitting as cheerfully as possible to its mishaps, our party came on its way.

Finally the city walls came into view, its battlemented outline showing through the veil of dust which hung over the city. Within the shadow of the massive gate towers we exchanged our precarious saddles for less uncertain sittings in staunch Peking carts. These carts seemed like large dry goods boxes on wheels, each cushioned and lined and set upon the shafts with an opening toward the front. As we approached the cart which was to carry us the carter sprang from his perch upon the shafts and, lifting the stiff cushion upon which he had been sitting, produced a short bench. Placing the bench upon the ground, one end against the cart wheel and his foot on the other end to steady it, he waited for us to mount.

From the bench to the shafts I climbed, then backing into the cart, was seated upon its cushioned floor. Drawing my feet under me, I made room for my companion, who backed in and took her place in front of me. The carter then took up his bench, put it into place, with its ends resting on the shafts and its legs projecting downward; then, letting the heavy cushion fall, he sprang upon the seat so formed, and with feet dangling took up the lines and we were off. It required constant adjusting on our part to keep our heads from coming into violent contact with the sides of the swaying cart, as the wheels, first on one side and then the other, descended into the deep ruts of the stone-paved way.

Passing through the city gate, our carter soon turned aside from the stone road, and then our cart rolled along comfortably enough. We passed through a place filled with mounds formed by the debris of former buildings. We were told that the houses once here were, years ago, razed to the ground, in order to rid

29

First home of the Woman's Foreign Missionary Society, Peking (1872–1886)

the city of a gang of robbers who infested this locality. Leaving this forsaken place behind, our carter turned into Filial Piety Lane and stopped before the gate of the Methodist Mission compound. Up and down the street as far as we could see were only dusty, gray brick walls, with here and there heavy doors closing the entrances to the houses which were behind the walls, but invisible from the street.

We crawled out of our carts and stood upon one of the great cubes of stone, two of which flank the gateway. Stepping down, we entered the great double gate, which was swung open by the gatekeeper, who made his bow as we passed, and stood within the walls of a brick-paved court. Beyond the walls of this gate court were three homes. Two were occupied by the two families then belonging to the North China Mission, and the third stood unoccupied, waiting the arrival of this new Mission's first representatives from the Woman's Foreign Missionary Society.

Well, we turned to the left and passed through another gate, and went to exchange greetings with the members of the family with whom we were to make our home until we could set up housekeeping for ourselves. Then, dusty and tired, we turned again and were shown through another gate into the house which was to be our home through so many changing years. Here we found a room fitted up for our present use.

Early in the morning of the next day, I stepped into the weed-grown court in front of our house. A great dog bounded forth, and in greeting placed his paws upon my shoulders, then dropping to the ground, he marked the entire length of my gown with two streaks of Peking mud. The act made an impression upon my mind as well as upon my gown, whereby I remember that it rained that April morning in Peking. A path through the weeds led to a hole in the wall. It was a perfect circle, about six feet in diameter, nicely finished in masonry—the Chinese moon-gate.

Nearby was a small building, then used for a chapel. Beyond that, and joining the court in which I stood, was another court which was to be used for our girls' school. From somewhere on the other side of the walls came the sound of voices united in a sing-song of unmeaning sounds. The boys of our mission school were studying their lessons in a room just over the wall. Turning about, I faced the little house in which we had spent our first night in Peking. There it stood under its heavy tiled roof. Three rooms in a row and a veranda across its length. It was a Chinese house which had been fitted with board floors and glass windows, and, like nearly all houses in Peking, was only one story high.

All this has changed with the sixteen years that have passed since then. The weeds, after a struggle, gave place to grass and shrubbery. The old wall, with its moon-gate, and the little chapel, were torn down, and beyond the old foundations a new wall was built, which wall joins the new and larger chapel over to the east, to bound the premises of the Woman's Foreign Mission Society. Still further to the east, and beyond a high wall, flourishes a boys' school, in large, well-appointed buildings, which school had its beginning in that school of street boys who shouted their lessons that rainy morning so long ago.

The size of our house was increased to more convenient dimensions, by throwing out a wing to the front and adding a kitchen to the back. Because of its peculiar dimensions our friends called the house the Long Home. Here Miss Brown and I set up housekeeping, and here we spent three happy, busy years together. Here we were joined by Dr. Combs (1873), who made her home with us until her house and hospital were built. Here Miss Campbell spent her short life of devoted labour (1875-1878), and here she died. With zeal, matched by the strong will with which she overcame all difficulties, and unsparing self-denial, she gave herself to the people with whom she had cast in her lot.

The few years of her missionary life were filled with incessant toil. And now she rests. In this same house we welcomed Dr. Howard (1877), and to this home came Miss Cushman (1878), bringing with her a quickening atmosphere of love and energy, and here Miss Cushman and I welcomed Miss Sears and Miss Yates (1880), and later Mrs. Jewell (1883).

The workers, who through the busy years made their home in that little house behind the walls of Filial Piety Lane, are widely separated now, and the little house is only a memory in the hearts of those who loved it for the associations of the years in which they called it home. The house was finally torn down (1896) to make room for the school, which, planted in the court to the east, grew until the eastern court was not large enough to contain it.

After Mrs. Gamewell had left us for her eternal mansion Mrs. G. R. Davis (Miss Maria Brown), who had shared with her the sacrifice, toil, and victory of those early days of the Peking Mission, in a letter of reminiscence, writes:

I do not recall that Mary ever told me in detail about her call to mission work, but I know there was a positive conviction that she was called to the foreign field, which did not yield to the repeated expression of opinion from three veteran missionaries, that our Mission Board had made a grave mistake in appointing us to Peking, as there was absolutely no work that a young woman could do there.

We came out the year after the Tientsin Massacre, when the prejudice against all foreigners was still very strong in the North. We rarely went on the street without seeing women placing their hands over the children's eyes lest we bewitch them.

"We were friends from our first meeting in San Francisco, and our close contact during the voyage strengthened the bond. We used to walk the deck together or lean over the side of the ship and sing softly, '*If on a quiet sea, toward heaven we calmly sail,*' but it was not a quiet sea on which we sailed in that late autumn of 1871.

We felt our first genuine touch of homesickness when we reached Shanghai. Many of our fellow-passengers were missionaries, returning from furlough, who lived in Shanghai, and the friends who crowded around to greet them in the joy of their greeting, impressed us with the consciousness that we were strangers in a strange land. However, there was welcome and greeting for us in the hearts and home of Dr. and Mrs. Lambuth. A few days with them, and, as the last steamer for the North had left the day before our arrival, we accompanied the Misses Beulah and Sallie Woolston to Foochow, and found a home and warm-hearted friends with Mr. and Mrs. Sites.

They were very kind to us during the three months of our stay in Foochow, and Mary charmed the children of the household with her singing. They had never heard the songs of the war until she sang them and they did enjoy them so much. We were unable to secure a Mandarin teacher there, but a Chinese teacher gave us lessons in writing character, and discouraged me with the assurance that I would never be able to equal her in excellence. Although we did not learn much Chinese, we did learn many lessons while in Foochow. We saw the work as it then was, and heard many stories of the early years, when faith not sight held the workers to the task they had undertaken, and we came North prepared not 'to despise the day of small things'!

We had been asked many times during our stay in the South: 'What do you expect to do?' We had always the one answer: 'Anything that we can find to do.' Our North China Mission was in its infancy. A beginning had been made. Our coming gave help and comfort to the other workers, if we could not at first take any part in the effort to reach our neighbours. Our home attracted the women who lived near, and we had many callers during the time when we could only smile and show them pictures and our various belongings in the effort to convince them that we were friends.

It was in our home, and at Mary's suggestion that she and I knelt each day at noon to ask God's blessing on the work. In some way Dr. Lowry heard the matter referred to, and urged that it be made a time for prayer for all the Mission. And so through Mary's influence was established the noon prayer meeting, which through all these years has been a power in our Mission for harmony and spiritual uplift.

Our home was very dear to us both. Mary insisted upon a division of household cares, and also that I was on no account to do any part of her tasks that she might chance to overlook. Nor would she suffer me to please myself by doing things for her, declaring that it would certainly foster selfishness. She was full of enthusiasm, and her bright young face, ready smile, and unfailing cheerfulness, made her a general favourite. We were happy in our home, but our work was like all pioneer work- hard and often discouraging. But the only thing that counted was that there really was work to do and work that was worth doing.

She still lives in the hearts of many for whom she laboured here, and the influence of her life and work must endure, a more lasting monument than the beautiful stone which marks the last resting place of the earthly tabernacle.

CHAPTER 5

In the Peking Compound

Life in the Methodist Mission compound in the city of Peking back in the seventies was very unlike that that triumphs there in this first decade of the twentieth century. In that area there are now many sweet homes, schools, a hospital, a university, and a splendid church, where hundreds of devout Chinese worship the true God and his Christ. The whole inclosure is pervaded by an atmosphere of intellectual culture, social refinement, and spiritual life, which is all the more vital because of the deadly heathenism with which it is contrasted. But this is the result of many years of patient and laborious toil, demanding a courage and sacrifice worthy that of the apostolic times.

Imagine a young woman who has felt the pulse of the nineteenth century, and one to whom the prize of distinction and large usefulness in her own land had been extended, shut in a little world in which are only eight of her countrymen. A gray brick wall twelve feet high bounds her horizon. Here are a few old buildings, not only foreign but Oriental; picturesque indeed with their tiled roofs and overhanging eaves curved up as if shrivelled by the intense summer heat, but ill adapted to American modes of life. The Chinaman's idea of home comfort and ours are as antipodal as are our tongues. The average American sleeps in a better room than the well-to-do official of China, who erects his house with no idea whatever of sanitation, and no idea of comfort as we understand comfort.

The missionaries had taken out the paper windows and substituted glass, and they had laid board floors above the brick pavement on which the original owner, though wealthy, was content to live. But still the entire aspect was Oriental, ever deepening the oppressive feeling of a far separation from home. The blue sky is much of the time obscured or dyed to gray by great masses of dust which lay on the city like a thick cloud. When the wind blows these dust clouds swirl and swish, penetrating every crevice of your home, and forcing the retreat of broom and duster in inglorious defeat. The dust, heavily laden with the poisons of a filthy city, penetrates your garments, scratches your skin, irritates your eyes. You breathe it, you taste it, you smell it. A rainy day is a boon. How unlike the spirit of our own land to speak of "a lovely rainy day"! Yet Miss Porter writes:

> The rain is pouring as if in haste to fill up the measure of the Peking rainy season, all in this one drenched Saturday. The dampness is like new vigour to nerves tight drawn through the long dry season of this climate. The seclusion of these dripping days is favourable to letter writing, and the patter, splash, rush, and pour make sweet music to time one's thoughts and one's pen.

All this is very interesting for a mere visitor who is there for a few weeks. Its novelty is a charm, and its very discomforts add spice to the spirit of adventure; but to make this one's life, day by day through long and weary years, is an endurance to test the stoutest courage.

When Miss Porter would seek relief by venturing outside the gates of the compound she is at once confronted by the gateless wall of race hatred, and cannot enter sympathetically into the life of the great world into which she has come with her message of love. She is physically repulsive to the Chinese. Her speech is barbarism. Her manner, measured by Chinese etiquette, is coarseness itself. What gentleman would be seen walking the streets with his wife? Children cover their eyes and run from her, screaming with terror till at a safe distance, when they will join with others in the cry, "Foreign devil!" Many look upon her as an intruder, and are bold to let her know that she is not wanted. They think her a meddler, coming to attack their venerable faith, and race hatred is intensified by religious passion. A young and sensitive woman must have hidden resources to endure all this and hold to her purpose. As it is, it is safer and pleasanter to keep as much as possible within the compound with her few companions, in spite of its limited range and its dusty old Chinese houses, so unlike her sweet home beyond the seas. Her earliest work was in the main preparatory. Under date of 1872 she writes:

> The friends here have been very kind, as we have found them everywhere. Mr. Wheeler in everything is thoughtful for our comfort; his kind heart appears in all his arrangements for us.

They had fitted up two rooms for us in the house that we shall occupy, and made every arrangement that could contribute to our comfort and make our future home seem more homelike. Our lot joins Mr. Wheeler's on the left and the school grounds on the right. Additions are to be made to our house, and the old building on the school lot is to be replaced by a new one. The two houses are to be connected by a covered passage. This work will not be done short of three months, perhaps.

The prospects for a school are encouraging. Three girls have asked admission. We would like to open school at once if there were only suitable buildings for it. The work of our mission has only just begun in Peking. The church membership is very small and includes no women. We shall have to employ a heathen woman as matron in the school, of course with the hope that she may be converted. Our teachers are all men. The women are very ignorant and unfit for teachers.

Daily routine of study and teaching without relief, threatens to become drudgery. And when to it we add the oppressive loneliness of wide and long separation from one's kindred, and the constant drain on one's sympathies which the woes of heathendom occasion, there is danger that it will irritate a fiery spirit till it finally becomes a nervous wreck. Many instances are reported. Miss Porter in one of her early letters refers to four missionaries of whom she knew, whose minds had utterly given way under the strain. The pressure is harder on young women than on those who are married, for these latter have diversion in the care of their families. It does ease one to shift the burden from one shoulder to the other.

Recreation, in the American sense, is practically impossible in the serious atmosphere of initial mission work. To seek diversion in some earnest study which does not bear directly upon the work is not regarded with favour, and when such study becomes absorbing it is openly condemned. "This one thing I do," though enforced by no statute, is the imperative law of our China Missions. If Miss Porter suffered the natural depression of her environment in those early days, we have learned of no statement of it from her lips or pen. Yet not to have suffered it would have been superhuman. But she had her conflict unknown to the world, alone in the wilderness of her temptation. She returned from her struggle a victor, and took up her work afresh with renewed strength. In a letter to one very dear to her, she says:

If I were not afraid that I should lose ground or grip by doing so, I would acknowledge to you that I carry about with me a sense of failure all the time, because of things that I do not get done. The secret is known between God and myself only. I put on a bold front and refuse to acknowledge *that there is anything I ought to do which I cannot do.*

She says the secret was her own. This is doubtless true of the details of her conflict; but the secret of her victory is apparent to all who knew her intimately. It was due partly to the robust healthfulness of her entire nature. She was in the fullness of physical health, and seems to have inherited much of her mother's reverence for the proper care of the temple of the Holy Spirit. She was removed by immeasurable spaces from the morbid view of the ascetic. Speaking of one whose mind had become unbalanced in his work, she says: "It all comes from unnatural modes of living: Chinese clothes, single life, and solitude." She adds:

The matter of how missionaries ought to live is often a question among missionaries themselves, and no one is supposed to have reached the perfect solution. I personally have settled in the common sense view of the North China Mission. The missionary who has the Spirit is always successful in winning and helping souls: and his home comforts do not lessen his usefulness. The only difference between the man who has the Spirit and lives poorly and the man who has the Spirit and lives comfortably is that the latter is likely to keep his health longer, and when it does break he knows it was not for lack of comforts which he might have had for the asking. It seems to me that the only thing for a missionary to do is to wait on the Spirit and keep the temple in as good repair as possible.

With this principle, she studied the matter of food, dress, and exercise with the same reverence and joy with which she would furnish and adorn the house of God. Another element of her strength was her healthful mental tone. The journals of those years reveal no taint of morbidity. She absolutely refused to let the walls of the compound, or even the great wall of North China, limit her vision. She kept herself informed on all the great movements in her own country and in the world. Her comments on the political and commercial events in America would have made creditable editorials for our great metropolitan journals. She was specially interested in all missionary efforts in all parts of the world, and studied them in their mutual relationship.

If we were asked to name what we reckoned to be the distinctive feature of her mind, we would say *breadth*. To such a mind there is no dull and cheerless and wearisome monotony. Even the mangled foot of a Chinese little girl has relations and significances widening out into the mysteries of the kingdom. She once said:

> Mary of Bethany little dreamed how great a thing she wrought when she poured that precious ointment on His person. But it is given us to know that in doing so little a thing as relieving a mangled foot we are doing that for Jesus which he calls 'this gospel, which shall be preached throughout the whole world.'

Another secret of her triumph was her inborn sensibility to Nature's touch which kept her heart ever fresh. In dust-clouded Peking there is very little of Nature to be enjoyed. But she found it. We have seen how the patter of the rain sent her pen on rhythmical meditations. She loved to walk out on the wall of the Tartar city to the observatory where she could get the most commanding view of the great metropolis and suburbs. In one of her earliest letters she gives this bit of description, which we repeat because of the glimpse it gives of her heart:

> This point commands the finest possible view of the entire city, though in its summer dress it looks more a forest than a city; and the thick foliage of innumerable trees, through which the yellow tiles of the palace building glimmer in pleasing contrast, overshadow the low houses and obstruct the view in all directions. The multitude of trees and birds is a great redeeming feature of this filthy city of dust and wickedness (that dust is near akin to wickedness all housekeepers will allow). The trees are inclosed in the walls by which all dwellings are surrounded, and we may not enjoy their shade; but we may walk on the city wall and enjoy the sight of their refreshing green, and breathe the pure air which perhaps has swept the very woods beneath whose shade we used to walk.
> The little birds that flit about our high-walled courts are constant visitors during both summer and winter, though the liveliest imagination cannot fancy that they, or those birds of loftier flight that fly shrieking through the air, ever saw America. It is but fair to add, all the birds do not shriek as they fly, only those that have whistles on their tails. These whistles are an ingenious

sort of wind instrument made vocal by motion through the air, as they speed their flight, on the tails of pet pigeons that fly at large in great numbers over all the city. The whistles are tied to the birds before they take their daily flight. The peculiar buzzing shriek can be heard in all directions and for some distance from the city, to the satisfaction of the peculiar inventive genius of the Chinese mind.

But the principal reason of her triumph over her depressing outward conditions was her communion with God. The following extracts from letters to members of her family reveal the secret of her strength:

No, I have had no regular—wonder if you did not mean irregular—fits of homesickness. I have longed to see you all, thought of you until the tears come—not common with me—but there is no despondency in it. I fully believe God has kept me from such feelings and in answer to prayer. I think I have told you how buoyed up I have felt at times when the most natural feeling would have been heavy sadness. An Influence has supported me all the way that I did not feel in past days. When I remember the promised prayers and the assurance from societies, Sunday schools, and churches that they are praying for me, it is no wonder. Prayer seems to me a more substantial comfort the older I grow, more like a real talk, and I know and see the answers to some of my prayers, and no doubt all are answered.

Now, in answer to your question, '*anxious* to be back' does not describe the state of my feelings. I am content to wait, but when the time does come for my visit home I think none could be more joyful. I long to see you all again. Sometimes I ache with the feeling of how impossible it is for me to see you now; but, my sister, I think God has given me a gift, a gift of faith that we shall be united on earth, to comfort me. I used to pray for you all with what was real agony because of my dread of what might happen, but for a long time that feeling has left me and a quiet sort of assurance takes its place, and I am content, and I do believe this assurance comes from God, that he who cares for us so carefully, kindly, wisely, thus prepares my heart for my work here.

When she consecrated herself to the work of a missionary it was with the full conviction that she was sent of Christ, and that his promise, "*Lo, I am with you alway*," was given to her personally. It is not to be supposed that at that time she fully understood the measure of the sacrifice and peril that her consecration would entail, but she never lost the strength of her conviction or the cheer of his presence. There came times when a tragic death was imminent, and others when death would have been a happy relief, yet never when in the prosecution of her legitimate work had she any fear. "Why," said she, "should I be alarmed when I know that He whom I serve is with me?"

That this courage was really due to the sense of Christ's presence when she was engaged in his service, appears from the fact that fear did distress her when peril came while she was engaged in some other work, however innocent, which was not strictly missionary. Once she went to see the celebrated spring at Chi Nan Fu, and came unexpectedly into peril. And then she suffered apprehension which she would not have felt if in the line of duty:

> The nearest way from the spring to our carts was through a large square, where on certain days there are markets, or fairs. So large a company is accustomed to gather at these fairs that it would not be thought safe for foreign ladies to appear there, and much more so since they are very seldom seen on the streets. On this particular day our friends thought there was no fair, and proceeded to take us through the square. Too late to turn back we discovered the square full of people, and a fair in full play. We passed about half way through without attracting the attention of the people busy with their own affairs. Before we had proceeded much farther attention was called to our presence by cries on every side.
>
> A multitude of idlers began to follow. People from the gates rushed out to swell the throng. They ran shouting: 'Foreign devils! foreign devils !' Then pausing, we could hear only the murmur of the great crowd following; then would come the rush of pressing throngs and fearful howls. As is the only safe and prudent way under such circumstances, we walked quietly and deliberately, not desiring to turn the affair into a chase, with no telling what disaster to follow. The walk seemed very long; and with that ever and anon howl in our ears it was not altogether free from apprehension, for a slight touch only is needed to turn an idle crowd into a howling, destructive mob.
>
> I think that if I had been on missionary business, instead of sightseeing, I should have felt not the slightest tremor of alarm.

As it was, I was not sure I was in my right place, and was glad when we reached our carts and were off through the gates once more.

This was a feature of her spiritual life which, while not unique as a fact, is rarely understood and interpreted as it was by her. The presence of Christ in the world is not simply a blessed memory of two thousand years ago, nor a sweet experience that is ours occasionally when we are in a suitable devotional frame. He is ever present personally in his work. To be heart and will in his work is to be in his presence. His omnipotence enfolds you. His love inspires you. With such a conviction, we can understand her courage which to other minds seems reckless, but which in the result is seen to be the power of God.

CHAPTER 6

School Work

The specific work assigned Miss Porter and those associated with her as representatives of the Woman's Foreign Missionary Society was to organise and maintain a girls' school and to do evangelistic work among women. To organize a school without a scholar, without apparatus, without the language, and without an acquaintance with the habits and mental attitude of the people, was a task almost hopeless. It would have been actually so only for the sublime faith of the young women who came to Peking under the conviction that the eternal God had sent them to do this thing. To their faith nothing was impossible. If Miss Porter had been able to cast her eye over the thirty-five years of her missionary life and foresee the splendid results as she did see them before she ended her earthly labours, she could not have begun her work with greater courage and zeal than she did that first morning after her arrival in the mission compound.

She saw the triumph from afar:
By faith she brought it nigh.

The following paragraphs from her pen give us admission into the schoolroom, and reproduce for us somewhat of its life, as the mere annalist could not possibly do.

On the ninth of April we took possession of our little house vacated for us by Mr. Davis and Mr. Pilcher. To this house they made an addition of one large room, and built beside it a small schoolhouse. In the following August (1872) we opened school with two pupils present.

The first little girl who came to our school ran away again as fast as her bound feet could carry her just as soon as she saw us. She had never before seen foreigners, and the first sight she found very frightful. The child was captured and brought back and put into the care of her aunt, who had been engaged as matron for the school to be. When the child had become reconciled to her new home her feet were unbound, she was bathed, and put into a suit of new clothes; and our school had its first pupil—Hui Hsin, we called—her one of seven who remained.

During the first year or two of the school's existence about sixty girls came and went away again; only seven came and remained. Those who brought children to the school generally brought them only that the school might relieve them of the support of the children. Then, when their fears were roused by silly tales about the foreigners, or their neighbours taunted them with having sold their daughters to the foreign devils,' they came and took the children away.

Sometimes the girls were left in school only long enough to get nicely clothed, and then were taken out of school and their clothes sold or pawned. In one case, which was followed up with a hope of saving the child, Miss Brown succeeded in making her way into a contracted, dingy room, where she found the little girl, who, a few days before, was in the school happy and well dressed, now shivering and miserable, with only the rags of some worn-out bedding for a covering. Her garments had been taken to the pawn shop by the wretched creatures who controlled the child's life.

In the years since its beginning the school has made a good reputation for itself, and a Christian church has gathered about the North China Mission. The difficulty of persuading people to leave their children after they had been received into the school has passed away, and the question now is how to make room for all who want to find a place in the school.

Lucy was one of our first girls. When I recall the school as it was in its first days, with seven little heathen girls, on whom we had so little hold because they had no lore or trust for us in their darkened hearts, and contrast it with the school that now is filled with Christian girls, who, on the right and on the left, hold up their teachers' hands, and whose influence is now felt strong and helpful through all our North China work, I feel sorry for those first girls.

It was in taking care of them that we gained that knowledge

of the Chinese character and mind which better fitted us for further work. On them we practiced our first stammerings in a strange language. Their opportunities are not to be compared with those that the school offers now, with its established precedents, its experienced teachers, and its wholesome Christian atmosphere.

Lucy was an only child of poor parents, and spoiled. A slender, graceful, wilful girl, with a quiet but keen face, who with low-voiced persuasion or cutting sarcasm held sway over her companions. She was fond of her books, but shirked, whenever possible, all duties demanding physical exertion.

Lucy was always ladylike in her bearing, and never came to open issue with her teachers; but her ready wit could find something to turn into ridicule for the amusement of her companions, in any task assigned her.

One day she was seated upon our sitting room floor, with a circle of younger girls about her. Her task was to prepare patches, and help the younger ones to mend a pile of clothing that lay before them. She did not look upon the task with any pleasure. While I was in another room, I overheard her saying in her usual quiet voice, as she held in view a roll of pieces of new cloth: 'Our teacher talks much about the Bible doctrine, and is continually exhorting us; nevertheless, she herself does not follow the Bible teaching. You see these new pieces and those old garments, and you all know that the Bible says you must not mend old garments with new cloth.'

Closely associated with this memory of Lucy is a picture of her mother as I last saw her. She was a tidy, brisk little woman, who tried to save her daughter at her own expense. She often did Lucy's washing which Lucy was supposed to do herself, and when the clothes were dried and neatly folded, she allowed her to bring them to me as the result of her own exertions. In the same way she tried to do Lucy's sewing for her. Then one day this mother, who in her mistaken kindness thwarted so many lessons intended for her daughter's good, sent word that she was ill and wanted to see me.

I found her in a room not much larger than the stove-bed upon which she was lying. She was flat upon her back, with her poor cramped feet drawn up, and notwithstanding her pain and weakness, with her hands extended upwards, she was at work on a pair of stockings for Lucy. The poor woman confessed that she had broken her promise to first consult me, and had betrothed Lucy, urging as a reason why I should be satisfied that she had found a professing Christian for a husband for her daughter.

She told me that she knew she was dying, and with tears besought me to complete the arrangements she had begun. She gave as a reason for breaking her promise, that she had an opportunity for marrying Lucy to a man whose mother was dead, and so she had settled the matter at once, that Lucy might be spared the trials of living with a Chinese mother-in-law. In a land where the husband's mother rules as she wills the life of her son's wife, even a heathen mother realizes the unhappy estate of a young wife. Dying, as living, this mother had no concern for herself, if only she could be assured of a comfortable settlement for her darling daughter.

The mother died and the daughter was married. Lucy was a professing Christian; but poor, spoiled child, she did not have the grace to make a very good wife. Lucy's husband was very proud of his bright, graceful girl wife; but his slower wit and uncontrolled temper put him at the mercy of her exasperating teasing. She laid traps for his temper, and he walked right into every trap. One day she tormented him into a rage. He, in the midst of his storming, told Lucy that the Bible teaches that the wife should obey the husband. She answered him that in her Bible there was no such word as 'obey.'

He in turn demanded that she bring her Bible and he would show her whether or not it contained any such word as 'obey.' For once Lucy was promptly obedient. The demand was what she had planned and worked for. The Bible was produced. The wrathful husband turned to Paul's epistle. Sure enough, there was no such word upon the page. Lucy had prepared for this scene. She had neatly encircled each objectionable little word with the sharp point of a pin, and one by one they had dropped out, and now the word was no longer in her Bible.

After a few troubled months Lucy became very ill, and they said she must die. She sent for one of her former teachers, who again directed her to the Lamb of God; and poor, erring Lucy at last entered into rest. She went from the arms of her teacher to the Saviour, who loves and cares more than we can love and care. '*A bruised reed shall he not break.*'

Another child there was whom we called Hui An. She was an odd child, and was in high favour with her missionary teachers, but nearly always in disgrace with the old Chinese teacher. She had unusual reasoning power, by which she comprehended our teachings better than the other pupils, and made application of what she understood to her individual life; but Hui An seemed to have little faculty for memorizing, so she was in disgrace with a teacher, whose teachings consisted in setting tasks for the memories of his pupils.

In the days when the school was small the girls used to come each evening, one by one, into a quiet room of our house, and kneel and repeat a prayer after me. One day, as soon as the girls were out of school, Hui An knocked at my door and asked, 'Please may I say my prayers now?' I told her she had better wait for the usual hour, but she stood there sorrowful and unwilling to go, and timidly repeated her request. She was very much in earnest, so, to her evident relief, I led her to the room and listened while she made her prayer. She got up from her knees with a satisfied and happy face. I again asked why she came at this hour.

By this time she had gained a little more courage, which courage seemed to have been taxed to the utmost in making the first request, and, standing upon one foot, toying nervously with her big sleeves, and with downcast face, she said: 'I love so much to play that every day I just play as hard as I can, from the time school is out until supper time, and after supper to prayer time, so when I come in to pray I just can think of nothing but the play, and all out of breath I want to rush through the prayer and be off to play again. And now,' she said, 'since I know that God knows about this kind of business, and don't like it, I am afraid to do so any more.' She went on to say that if she prayed before she played, she could say her prayers and think about what she was saying, so she came as soon as school was out to have the prayers all right. We were very happy over this token that God was working in the hearts of our girls.

Years after, when this little girl was grown, and there were many Christians among our girls, we found the girls in a room where quite a number slept, working a plan by which they secured opportunity for private devotions. When the retiring bell rang, the girls took down the pile of quilts that occupied one end of the long stove-bed. Then each girl folded her quilt and betook herself, feet first, into the snug pocket so formed. When all were disposed side by side, feet to the wall and heads out, one of the larger girls put out the light. This was the signal for all talking to cease. Immediately all the girls lying there in a long row raised their voices in a hymn. The singing ended; then all was silent, while each girl covered her face and breathed her prayer to the Father they had learned to love since they first learned to fear him. 'We love him because he first loved us.'

One year from the time when Maria Brown and I sat at study by a wood fire in southern Foochow we sat in Peking before a stove in which burned a coal fire to keep out the cold of a northern winter. Then we were studying the language; now we were considering certain questions which ever since our arrival in Peking had been thrusting themselves more and more into view and could no longer be ignored. We had come in from a Sunday evening service held in the home of a neighbouring mission and sat before the fire in the quiet of a Sabbath night, facing those questions that we might now meet and settle them once for all.

Always, when I look down the years that have passed since the year 1872, to memory's picture of that little sitting room in Peking and those two sitting in the lamplight there, the picture seems to glow with the soft radiance of a Divine Presence. And as, instructed by the experience of the intervening years, I realize the far-reaching results of that night's decisions, and how limited the experience and powers of those who made them, my heart thrills with the glory of a sure conviction that the Almighty Master was one in the conference that night, that his Spirit guided our minds, and the decisions were his very own.

The questions decided were, should or should not the feet of girls admitted to our school be unbound? And what should be the limit of our intercourse with our brethren among the missionaries? Nowhere else in China were the feet of girls in mission schools being unbound. Some missionaries thought the movement to unbind the feet hurtful to the progress of the gospel. And we had been told that if we undertook to unbind the feet of pupils, we should never be able to establish a school for girls in China. Already some of our little band of pupils had been taken away because we had unbound their feet.

The leaders of our Mission were men of vision, judgment, and faith. They were young and had the enthusiasm and courage to give full swing to conviction and make no compromise with expediency. The knowledge that we could count upon their support greatly strengthened our purpose. We decided to unbind the feet, and in so doing emphasize our teaching that the body is the temple of the true God and must not be profaned. Then we should leave the results with the God whom we tried to honour before a heathen people.

As to the second question, we had seen a genteel old lady, whose respect we prized, hurry in scandalized agitation from our room because she had seen us shake hands with a gentleman who appeared at our door while she was present. By this and other signs we had become aware that our reputations were at stake among a people whose conception of the possibilities of womanhood is limited by the assumption that womankind are upright only so far as they lack opportunity to be otherwise.

The presence of single women in China missions was an offense against all Chinese ideas of propriety. Their position was beset by embarrassments and perplexities; and so serious were the embarrassments and perplexities attending their presence that there were missionaries on the field in those pioneer days who believed the introduction of single women workers into China missions to be a mistake.

In conference that night Miss Brown and I agreed that we should be misunderstood no matter what course we might choose, and that any attempt which we might make to conform to Chinese ideas of propriety in our intercourse with other members of the Peking circle not only would not abate the offense which our presence gave but would promote misunderstanding. We decided, therefore, that we should conduct ourselves in all our relationships according to the conventions of our own Christian land and trust to future developments to win for us the respect and confidence, without which we could not hope to teach and lead the people to whom we had come. There is evidence of divine guidance in the fact that we were brought to these decisions about the time that our infant

Methodist Church of North China was born. Through these decisions, supported by the hearty cooperation of the brethren, the infant church grew up familiar with the sight of girls with unbound feet, and familiar with lessons concerning the sanctity of the body as the temple of God, which the unbinding of the feet emphasized; and familiar also with the sight of men and women associating and counselling and working together on terms of equality and respect in the home, the school, and the church; and so the new church grew into new ideas concerning the dignity of womanhood and the possible partnership of womanhood with manhood for the benefit of both.

While the infant church was growing the girls' school, with its pupils with unbound feet, was growing; and it grew to be the largest girls' school in China.

CHAPTER 7

Unbound Feet

While at Foochow Miss Porter observed the crippled feet of the Chinese women, and studied them with a growing feeling of horror and shame. To her mind it was immeasurably more than a national fashion sanctioned by immemorial habit. It was a distinctive mark of the heathendom of that land, cruel, degrading and wicked. It was a desecration of the temple of the Holy Ghost, the defilement of which meant destruction. Its original purpose was not, as later ages claimed, to beautify the form divine, but to subject woman to the brutal tyranny of man. For a Christian to even tolerate it where her will could prohibit it, was for her to burn a pinch of incense on the altar of a heathen deity.

Thus it became a matter of conscience with Miss Porter; and when she began the organization of a girls' school in Peking she, with Miss Brown, firmly insisted on a rule that no girl be admitted until she had unbound her feet. This was a rule that had never been enforced in any school in the country. Wise men gravely doubted its wisdom, and counselled that concession would be expedient and more speedily accomplish the purpose of the rule. Moreover, is not that the divine law which casts off evil not by assaults from without, but by the unfolding of truth from within? She was told that this was a custom deep-rooted in the thought and heart of the people, and that her attempt must necessarily end in failure. Then to concede after the attempt, would be regarded everywhere as a surrender of Christian conscience to heathen principle; and that would be to wound the body of Christ in a vital part.

To all this she replied: "If the gospel we are commissioned to preach is equal to meet the deep-rooted depravity of the human heart, is it unequal to meet a single outshoot of that root? If this is simply a social habit, a matter of taste or even a weakness of judgment, then we are at liberty to concede. But this is a sin, and no more to be tolerated in our school than the sacred images."

Her enthusiasm and faith, supported by the strength of her reasons, triumphed. The missionaries heartily agreed to admit no girls in the school with bound feet. The following paragraphs are fragments gathered from various publications and letters from her pen:

A woman from an old and respected family, who bears herself with the dignity and complacency of a queen, gave herself and her family to God. She brought her two daughters a distance of four hundred miles to put them to school. Being fully convinced that foot-binding is a sin against the Creator and his children, she expected to have her daughters' feet unbound. The new shoes and stockings were brought forth and the process of unbinding began. Then, to the surprise of those who beheld, and probably to the surprise of the old lady herself, a struggle set up in the mother's heart—a struggle between the forces of old customs and prejudices and the power of the new faith.

Though at first she smiled in happy recognition and said, 'God's will be done; let the feet be unbound,' a moment later some power from the past caught away the smile and left a face twitching with emotions and followed by slow tears. With sighs and wringing of hands she walked across the floor to return and beg: 'Unbind only the feet of one and let the other child's remain bound.' Then reproaching herself, she took up her restless walk. Finally, she stood still and said with earnest, sober face: 'Go on; it shall be done.' Thus ended one of the many contests brought in by contact of a heathen purpose with a Christian principle—a Christian principle held by the women who opened a girls' school in the Methodist Episcopal Mission, Peking, in 1872.

The principle might be stated thus. It is a sin to crush and deform the feet that God gives to his children. We missionary teachers will not make ourselves party to this sin by appropriating missionary funds for the support of children with bound feet whose parents will not forsake this particular sin. Other little girls toddled into school and were freed from the cruel bandages. They came with stunted bodies, pinched features, and pale faces. After a while they found the use of their released feet, and running and playing in the open air as they never before were able to do, they gained in vitality, then flesh, and, again, rosy cheeks and bright eyes. In many cases the children changed so markedly within only a few weeks that their relatives failed to recognize them and were perceptibly impressed when assured that the change was due to release from the bandages.

There were Chinese preachers who for years sought places in schools for their daughters with bound feet, then finally yielded before the steady pressure of the principle and unbound the feet of their girls. Then, first to excuse themselves to the unbelieving, and finally from conviction, they began to preach earnestly against foot-binding.

Mighty changes have been wrought in and by the Peking Girls' School since 1872, when its first pupils five little Chinese girls gathered from heathen homes went because they had fallen into the hands of barbarians, who, as they said, 'do not know enough to know that we are only girls and can't learn books.' We were warned that we could never succeed in establishing a girls' school in China if we should undertake to unbind the feet of the pupils. Nevertheless, supported by the leaders of our mission, we decided to do this as a service due the true God whose temple the body is, and to leave the results to him whom we thus tried to honour before a heathen people.

The school grew slowly at first; but after a few years its development was rapid, and it took the place which it has held for years as the largest school for girls in China.

The best result of the unbinding of feet in the Peking school was not foreseen by the missionaries. The girls, by submitting to this break with established custom, were brought into heavy trials costing them pain and mortification. But these long-continued trials firmly borne developed strength and independence of character. They learned to think and act for themselves. The result was a steady, strong uplift to girlhood and womanhood which in turn carried upward the manhood of the church as well. They were the undaunted leaders in a movement which brought upon them and all other girls in the school, much suffering through evil report.

The girls of the Peking school returned from their first vacation. Among others were Clara and Sarah Wang (Sarah Fawcett

53

Wang). Clara and Sarah were girls of about thirteen and eleven years of age. They wept bitterly, and said that never, never did they wish to go home again. They had been made to suffer many indignities and insults because they had come into their native village with unbound feet, where girls with unbound feet had never before been seen, and now they never wanted to go home again.

We told them of the difficulties of all new beginnings, and how much they could help all who should come after them if they could have the courage to bear the brunt of pioneer work in these new beginnings. And we appealed to them in Christ's name: 'Can you not do this for his sake? Will you not help his cause by bearing this hardship? Go home every vacation and tell your villagers that it is for love of a new-found God and a precious Saviour that you remove the bandages which deform the body which he claims for his temple. Keep on telling, and after a while they will understand; and you will have served your Saviour and made things easier for all other girls who shall unbind their feet.' Those girls responded to such an appeal like soldiers to the bugle call, and never after did they complain. They went their way on their unbound feet a way which led to many another break with ancient customs which lay across the path of Christ's gospel. *So our young girls helped. . . . .*

The growth of the girls' school kept pace with the growth of the infant church and with that of the boys' school, now the Peking University. Many girl graduates are now the wives of preachers and teachers who have been fitted for work in this university. When opportunities for making money have tempted the young men graduates from the teacher's chair and the pulpit, such girls as Sarah Wang have steadied their husbands and saved them to the church by the force of the character whose development began while they stood resolute under the scorning poured upon them because of their unbound feet.

Dr. Rachel Benn has prepared for publication an account of a visit to An Chia Chuang, the old home of the Wangs in Shan Tung, in which she says:

Clara Wang, one of Miss Porter's and Miss Brown's earliest pupils came to visit me at my room, and upon hearing of the serious illness of Mrs. Gamewell, expressed great sorrow and anxiety, and then talked long and lovingly about her friend and teacher. 'From the time I entered her school,' she said, 'till she went back to her own country the last time, Mrs. Gamewell has been my *ting hao peng yu* (very dear friend) and helper. If she should die, I shall be bereft indeed, for I have no other friend like her. Mother took my younger sister Sarah and me on the wheelbarrow with her when she went to Peking, and unbound our feet and put us in the girls' school. There were but nine pupils then.'

To my question, 'How many years ago was that?' she replied: 'About thirty-one years.' 'Thirty-one years !' I exclaimed, 'and see what has come to pass in that time. Think of all the girls who have had their feet unbound, become Christians, become educated, married Christian men, and built Christian homes since then. Then look at our Peking school now.'

'Yes,' she replied, her eyes glowing, 'and the T'ai An school, too. Seventy-five pupils, and many more wanting to come. And this school work I commenced by Mrs. Gamewell's setting me to work when my husband and I came here to live.'

I told her of how, when I came here in 1893 with Mrs. Gamewell and others, she told me how she started the school, and added: 'That school is one of my treasures. Clara Wang was one of my first pupils, and I have always loved her.' And now, when the faithful teacher, tireless missionary, and loving friend has laid down her task and gone to her Father, how dear to find in a re-mote country village, a pair of hands she has trained and a heart which she has filled with love, going on with the good work!

The success of the movement in Peking, not only in the growth of the school, but also in its influence on the personal character of the girls themselves, greatly encouraged the Christian schools throughout the country to adopt and enforce the same rule. Who can tell what influence it may have had on the imperial government which has recently issued a decree commanding the unbinding of the feet of all women throughout the empire?

CHAPTER 8

First Country Tour

It is the policy of our Mission in Peking, as elsewhere, to extend its work as rapidly as its means will allow into all the villages and towns of that section of North China where other Protestant missions are not already established. It could not be otherwise, for it is the genius of the gospel to extend itself abroad; and our work multiplied far beyond our means to meet its demands. Many souls lighted their torches at the central altar and then went with its flame into all the regions round about, and came into the shadow of the great wall and beyond. While this created a promising opportunity for our missionaries, it also brought its perils. Many of these new converts had the most crude conceptions of Christian doctrine, which, combining with their superstitions and their heathen habit of thought, would, unless corrected, create a most untruthful and hurtful popular idea of the gospel. It was very needful, then, for our leaders to make up for their lack of numbers in doubling their energies, and literally to make "an offering of themselves for the people."

Our Mission, which began more than thirty years before the Boxer outbreak in 1900 with but two missionaries and their wives, and which at the time of Miss Porter's arrival had not one female convert, is now an Annual Conference with sixteen missionaries and their families from the Missionary Society of the Methodist Episcopal Church, and eleven missionaries representing the Woman's Foreign Missionary Society, eighty-two native preachers and a membership including probationers of six thousand. Our most distant station is about four hundred miles from Peking. In pursuance of her work, it became necessary for Mrs. Gamewell to make occasional itineraries to these distant stations. Her first tour to Tsun Hua, eighty miles from Peking, was made in 1880, two years before her marriage. She says:

The object of this trip was threefold; we very much desired to meet the women of our country charges and establish work among them. Then we think the best way to find women for our training school we hope to establish, is to go into the country and look for them among the women of the churches. Finally, so much disturbance has been raised about the girls brought to Peking from Tsun Hua District that we felt it best to send them home for the summer; but feared to lose them if foreign ladies could not go too and counteract as much as possible the reports in circulation.

While in the first instances these journeys were a relief from the routine of school work in Peking, and she wrote copious journals of the novel situations, and sketched a number of portraits of the interesting characters she met, the trips proved to be wearisome both to body and mind. At times even her hopeful spirit seemed to tremble under its weight of oppression. The novelty soon wore off, and only the great burden of heathendom lay heavily upon her heart. Every moment of her time was filled with exhausting efforts to relieve it with the limited means at her command. Were it not for the fact that she knew the secret of the Lord, the holy place of communion where he reveals his covenant to those who fear him, she would have sunken sick and faint. From the journal of her first country trip, made in 1880, we give a number of extracts in the order of their record.

In the next chapter we give selections from her other journals, the last of which was written in 1883, with no purpose of preserving chronological or topographical order. Our object is not to give a history of a country or a mission, or of any particular itinerary, but simply to afford a glimpse of a loving heart trying to bring the light of the gospel into benighted heathen minds. It is due to Mrs. Gamewell to say that these notes were never made with an idea of publication, but were hastily written for personal friends in the rush of a wearisome itinerary.

On the morning of the seventh of July [1880] we passed through the great gate and left the city for our first country trip. Miss Barr, of the Presbyterian Mission of this city, Mrs. Wang (a Bible woman), four young girls going home for a vacation, and myself made up our party.

The conveyances were carts, one of which was for the woman and girls, drawn by three mules. One of the mules was harnessed between the shafts, the other two attached by means of cable ropes, fastened on or near the axle. These ropes left the animals free to pull or roam at will over the country, through a circle of which they form the *radii*. However, these meanderings are divested of comfort by means of a whip resembling a fishing pole and line, handled by the carter. Another cart was provided for Miss Barr and myself. Into this we packed our bedding. Oriental inns do not provide beds; travellers carry their own, and much prefer to do so. We also put in our cart our satchels, books, and many other things.

On the back of the cart was strapped a large box containing dishes, kitchen utensils, and food. In the front was left sitting room for the carter and both of us, though in fair weather one was to ride the white pony, all saddled and bridled and made secure behind the cart, to trot along at his ease until wanted for more active service. Two mules drew our cart—a large creature belonging to a Presbyterian doctor of divinity, and a little Methodist mule in the ropes. Our little Methodist mule, however, often fell from grace and wandered most perversely, often entangling the feet of our Presbyterian mule in the ropes. Perhaps something concerning the perseverance of the saints may have confused her doings, for certain it is that whenever our Methodist mule meandered or capered, our mule of Presbyterian training *took a stand*. In many a rut she perseveringly stood until we were quite convinced that if we were not saints we needed to be.

We were overtaken on our first day out by a heavy rainstorm, which prevented us making as long a stage as we expected. We crossed two ferries, forded one river on a beautifully pebbly bottom, saw much beautiful country with broad fields and standing harvests, passed through little villages, and found good inns all the way. On Saturday the tenth we entered the mountain region, and from then till our arrival in Hsin Tien Tzu that evening our road lay through the most beautiful country I have seen in North China.

A cordial welcome was given us by the members of our little church in Hsin Tien Tzu, and especially by the family of Mr. Yang, in whose court the little chapel is situated. In this chapel we bestowed ourselves and our goods, purposing to make our home there as long as we stayed. One of the girls we brought with us is a daughter of Mr. Yang. It was pleasant to see the joy her return made in that Chinese home. A crowd soon collected about us, and it was an hour or more before we were allowed to change our clothes or refresh ourselves by washing our faces. But finally the crowd left, and we cooked and ate our evening meal. After that Mrs. Yang went with me to take two of the other girls to their home nearly four miles away. We found the girls' parents in their little house in the midst of green fields near by a melon patch and a deep cool well. The father brought out a bench and set it in the shade, spread a covering of coarse cloth over, and brought us sweet little melons from the field nearby, and water fresh from the well for us to drink.

The sun had gone down behind the purple shadowed mountains when we took our leave. The fields are not such patches as we see about Peking. Many cornfields join over invisible boundaries and give the appearance of large fields like those in the States; so also the grain fields. The hum of insect life, the twitter of birds, the cool, bracing air, the broad fields are like *home*—the first time that anything in China has seemed worthy of a comparison with the noble, inspiring, bracing sweetness of country living at home. This likeness to home—the steadfast hills, the quiet summer sky, the still hush of closing day, the honest, cordial people—all impress me till I am more spontaneously happy than since the happy-go-easy days of long ago.

By and by Mr. Yang met us at a turn in the road with a long open cart. We all got in, with the girls and the boys in a merry mood, who chatted and laughed all the way through, very much like young people at home—very *unlike* anything I had seen before in impure, untrue China. They seemed, as Miss Cushman would express it, 'like folks.'

The cool twilight ride through dewy harvests yet standing, helped the happy illusion, and I could almost imagine the years rolled back again, and I a light-hearted schoolgirl going for a vacation to the old familiar farmhouse. The new moon, a beautiful crescent, looked over my shoulder out of a sky yet tinged with the golden hues of sunset. And it was my right shoulder too!

At Hsin Tien Tzu the pastor asked me to take charge of the Sabbath service. They brought me the Bible and hymn book, and men and women gathered in little companies, asking me to teach and pray with them. So it came to pass after the beautiful Saturday already mentioned that I entered upon a Sabbath full of work.

Almost as soon as it was light the first comers entered. After breakfast I talked to the women who came until service time. Then, when Christians from all points of the country around had come in, we held service, I reading and talking and praying. Afterward I held class meeting. All the men spoke. There were a few earnest, honest faces there that made me feel that it was worth coming a hundred miles to see them, so unlike the wily faces everywhere seen previously. There were evidences everywhere of patient, faithful work by the missionaries and their helpers, the native preachers and teachers.

We took our way over the mountains to Wang Shu Chuang Tzu. We reached a pass high among the mountain peaks and began to descend. The view was refreshing and delightful beyond all description to eyes long accustomed to dusty Peking and its dirty environs—all about us the clear mountain air, near at hand moist banks of dripping grass and shrubs, and just below, fields of abundant harvests with all their varying shades of refreshing green, and here and there a grove.

All around the plain were encircling mountains, peak on peak rising higher and higher until their sharp outlines cut and pierced through sombre clouds which hung all around the horizon. Awesome and grand the steadfast masses lifted against the changeful sky, always the same strength and majesty, whether swept by the shadow of the soft summer cloud that floats in fleecy folds up its rocky sides or stormed by the hurtling thunderbolts of the tempest cloud in its awful grandeur and sublimity.

In the valley we found the little village. Men and women came to see and hear, though one might think, judging from their manner, that a foreign lady could be seen any day coming over the mountains in sight of these villagers. I was talking to the women, and after some time rose to go into the next room, when I found that a company of men and boys had collected and were sitting quietly on benches ranged near the door where I had been sitting.

One woman said abruptly, pointing to a sun-browned farmer sitting near: 'That man used to pray a lot, but he prays none now.' The man flushed a little and remarked in explanation that his crops were worse than his heathen neighbours,' and that did not look like getting anything in answer to his prayers. He insisted that he deserved better things because he prayed much. He evidently had more of the heathen idea of prostrations and humiliations to please the gods than the Christian idea of prayers.

After some talk I told him of a little boy who never tried to mind his father, never cared to know what his father wanted him to do. One day, being asked if he were a good son, he replied: 'Indeed I am. I am always asking my father for good things.' He was interested and pleased. The carter took up the subject, and talked well, too. Finally the man said: 'Enough, enough. I will begin again.' Here again we had reading and prayers.

I reached Peking after an absence of ten days, and thus ended my first country trip, which I hope will be succeeded by many more. Such trips have not been made by ladies in this part of the country, and many were anxious, not knowing what might befall us on the way. But we felt the sure presence of God before, around, and *everywhere*. We were well received; no crowds or impudence at inns; cordial welcomes everywhere from natives. We believe many friends have been made, much evil speaking quieted, and our women assured by seeing us whom their heathen neighbours had declared had no existence.

If I have written much about the scenery, it is because it was a constant inspiration to me. Something was constantly saying: '*The Hand that spread the plain and piled the mountains is making a plain path before you.*' '*Lo, I am with you alway*' seemed to breathe in the air all about us. The quiet heights by which we were surrounded, and the throng that came at daybreak, and left with the close of day, reminded me so often of the words spoken respecting Christ: 'He went up into a mountain apart to pray.' I realized that our only place of quiet rest would be the hills and mountains. The reminder brought Christ, his work, and spirit very near through those short, busy days.

There was rest in the glimpse we had through our window of a distant mountaintop, seen above the roofs of mud houses near at hand. I could not be impatient with the throng in sight of this reminder of those other throngs of long ago, and of how Christ met them and found his only rest among the solitudes of the mountains, where he prayed and prepared for toil yet to be endured.

CHAPTER 9

Country Evangelism

Except on the main roads, the inns are dirty and forlorn in the extreme. All we have put up in during this trip have been much alike in dirt and cheerlessness. We are just in from a long, hard ride in the cold. We may have a large room or a small one, well smoked, begrimed, and dusty, with a greasy table well coated with dust, a chair and bench, an earthen floor, a frame with four legs for a bed. The bedding must be provided by the traveller. Chinese and foreigners all carry their own beds. In some inns toward the South, and all in the North, the provision for beds is a brick platform built across one end of the room. Often men come into crowded inns and sleep on a bench in the court, or in any available place. To sleep among the animals in a Chinese inn is a much different matter from sleeping in a hotel stable in the United States or any other Western country. These inns in their Oriental style remind me of the Scripture narrative of Mary and Joseph stopping in the stalls, or stables, as implied by the statement that the Babe was laid in a manger because there was no room for them in the inn.

In China the rooms for travellers are arranged about one or more courts. The stalls for animals are in the same court, and carts, barrows, donkeys, horses, and everything that puts up in the inn, enter the same gate and share a common court. The rooms for travellers are bare of everything except a table and bench or two.

I arrived at the little mud village of Shang Chia Chai at five o'clock in the evening. A little cook stove in the chapel and an iron bedstead in the little room adjoining add to our comfort home luxuries much above those to be had at the inns along the road. To be sure, the floors are paved with dirt-coloured bricks, the windows are paper, the seats are benches without backs, plus three native chairs that offer as little comfort as chairs can be made to offer. Indeed, with high legs, shallow bottom, and high backs curved away just where one's back wants to feel support, and curved toward the occupant just at the nape of the neck, these chairs seem designed to thwart all expectations of ease. But the cook calmly sets to work and gets a supper, quite such as we might produce from our Peking kitchen. We sleep soundly in our little rooms about ten by eight feet, and feel happy, and call ourselves exceedingly well off to have such comforts so far from home.

On Saturday I took one of the Bible women and went to spend the day with the family Li in a village about one and a half miles away. I carried some sewing in my ulster pocket and employed my hands and eyes on it while resting my throat and head from an hour or two of talking to a large company of women and girls who crowded the rooms and court. I also took a lunch in my pocket, thinking thus to provide against making my host and hostess feel that they must prepare food for me. Poor as they may be, and cost what it may, every Chinese house one visits must give something to eat, or else offend against the commonly received ideas of hospitality.

My preparations would not release them, nor likewise my protestations. A meal was served me, and I had to eat in order to assure the little woman who prepared it that I was not afraid it was unclean. I could not give up the idea that in visiting the various villages that encircle our Mission station at Shang Chia Chai, I should accomplish more if I stayed all day and gave the noisy crowd time to tire and leave and give opportunity to talk quietly with the few than if, as before, I talked an hour or two to the crowds and then left. For my other visits I have added to my roll of sewing a parcel of lunch, still another parcel, a gift of cakes, fruit, rice, etc., for each family. So whatever they feel they must provide for me, I shall not leave them poorer for my visit. This carrying of gifts of such nature is quite in accord with the usual Chinese custom.

In this place our members are very fond of singing. Indeed, they love singing everywhere; but this place is an exception in that they sing well. Every night this little room rings with hymns. Some are the old, old hymns of the ages. Many are Sankey's and others like them.

The helper's wife brought her baby and came to hear the singing. She remarked that her husband was at home with the children, though he had wanted to come, for he said he could follow the teacher and learn the tunes! The hymn book is the most popular book in the church.

Sabbath dawned bright and beautiful. By noon the people had gathered from various neighbouring villages. The helper conducted a Sabbath school and preached. In the afternoon I held a meeting with the few Christian women who could remain. In the evening we did not omit the usual singing.

Monday morning I took a cart for a place four miles away. Here they were expecting our arrival, according to promise made last Sunday. The people who immediately filled the rooms were quiet and orderly, and listened as if that were what they came for. Their faces were lighted with interest, and it seemed as if Christ was really not far-off . As I said to one who questioned by look and tone, 'Why, if you really want his help, Christ is even now close by your side. He looks into your heart. He hears your words. He longs to have you believe and follow him,' it seemed as if he breathed upon us.

I thought of Bishop McCabe's words to the effect that at the moment when we are engaged for the saving of a soul the unseen powers of the other world are gathered to work with us for the same object, that such moments are the crises for the souls for whom we labour. The thought that the burden of longing for souls I felt was shared by pure unseen spirits, sent for the salvation of these same souls, that the compassionate face of Christ looked upon us and waited the issue, flooded me with a sudden sense of help and unworthiness. I was glad to hear Mrs. Li take up the story, while I hid my face under my hat for the tears that would come. Was Christ sorrowful as when the young man of many possessions turned away, or did his divine vision see the springing up of seed in good soil, the dawning of light in darkness, that comprehended it at least in part?

The second day out from Chu Chia Chai, we came to the Yellow River. We had heard that it had overflowed its banks and that the roads were impassable. And they also reported that it was impossible to enter Chi Nan Fu, as the water covered the approach to every gate. Mr. Lowry, having had large experience with Chinese reports, determined to 'go and see.' Accordingly, we came to the banks and found the river within bounds at the ferry, a little out of our usual way, and the water quite covering the roads below the point at which we crossed.

The inn at the place we came to was not so large as usual, and moreover, was full. After some delay an old and unoccupied shop was opened to us, and carts, horses, and mules all entered the same door. Animals were tied in the court behind the house, and carts, carters, and people all put up in this one dark, windy old shop. Mr. Lowry slept on the counter. Mrs. Lowry and I made a resting place on the *k'ang* in one end of the room. The carters stowed themselves away somewhere in or behind the carts. We extinguished our lights, and the utter darkness furnished a dressing room for the little change we made in our clothing.

At break of day we took some bread and butter from our basket and then took ourselves to the river bank. It was two and one half hours before we began to cross the muddy and swift-flowing current. The stream is so swift that boats cannot go directly over, but, pushing off, they pull for the opposite shore with might and main, and succeed in landing about a mile below the starting point. When ready for the return trip they scull and pole along the bank until at the proper distance above the desired landing on the other side, and then put out again, as in the passage over. The boats look much like our common flat-boats or coal barges. Planks are laid from bank to boat, animals un- hitched, carts pulled over planks by men, animals made to jump on, foot passengers walk on and stow themselves anywhere they may find standing room. Boatmen pole off and a man at the stern plies the scull. We crossed the river on Saturday morning and early in the afternoon were welcomed by missionaries of the Presbyterian Board in Chi Nan Fu.

After a journey of one hundred and eight miles we reached this place (Yang Chia Ying). We had spent two weeks at our former stopping place, and felt somewhat at home. Now we arrive at a new point and must begin our work over again. The fire must be lighted, the dusty contents of the cart deposited. The visitors come to 'open their eyes,' as the Chinese saying is when one goes sight-seeing. So we, all dusty and tired, land with our dusty baggage in a dusty room, rapidly filling with the dusty inhabitants of the dusty village. This one room, in constant use as a meeting room, must be our sleeping room, dining room, kitchen, reception room, and still be used as a chapel.

We had eaten last at 9:30 a. m., and supper was not ready until 8 p. m. However, the helper and wife and other members of the little church gave us a cheery welcome, and with a little time and care we finally settled comfortably. A shawl separates one end of the room from the rest; and here we feel somewhat more retired, and, consequently, more restful.

Three bright little girls came in to recite to me the lessons they have learned with Mrs. Chao, the helper's wife. The girls are older than they look, eleven, twelve, and fifteen. They have been coming in at odd times for almost one year, coming when they were not obliged to work. They recited the *catechism* almost all through, one tract and part of a book on faith—all these committed to memory. After they finished I gave each two pictures cut from an illustrated paper, and they seemed much pleased.

This morning Mrs. Li the elder and Mrs. Li the younger left for their homes, four days' journey from this place. I shall not see them again until they come up to school next autumn. I got up in the dim morning to see them start off in a slow rain. I came in feeling lonesome and half homesick. So partings haunt the days that follow in their train.

We went to a village four miles away to see a woman who was interested and had joined the church on probation. We found the room and court swept as tidy as possible. After a long talk, and we had prepared to leave, I called attention to a paper god hanging on the wall, and said: 'Such things should not be in the house of a believer in the true God.' I heard a woman of the company whisper to the women whom I addressed that the visitor might take down the gods for her, and then nothing could hurt her! Upon this she turned to me hopefully and asked if I would take them down for her. I did, and brought them away with me.

This was repeated a day or two after at another house. At a meeting held on the following Sabbath these women were present. One of them told how she had no fear of the displeased gods until night, and then in the dark she thought what if the two were there and should beat her. She thought of it until it seemed that they were really there. Then she said: 'I am not afraid, I am not afraid, for *my lady* has come.' She said: 'I just talked right out loud, as if someone was in the room, and then I felt my fear gone and went to rest.'

She told this as God's mercy to her. She is in the very first stages of knowledge of God's existence. Her faith which led her to use the little knowledge she had seemed very touching. Of course I told her how Jesus was near, and to speak to him when fear came, to tell the evil spirits that Jesus had come rather than that the lady had come.

Yesterday our party returned from a visit to Nan Kung, the county seat. We had heard from the helper that there were some interesting and interested persons there, who wished to hear more of the doctrine. We went up one day and returned the next there and back a journey of about forty-five miles.

We reached Nan Kung inn at 2 p. m. Our helper went out, while we prepared our dinner, to find the people whom we came to see. The first step in preparing our meal was to get from the cart a pan that has a perforated bottom and stands on three legs. In this we made a fire of charcoal. We boiled rice in a fruit can brought for the purpose, boiled potatoes in a butter can, made coffee in a pot of tin not larger than a good sized fruit can, sliced some roast beef, and took a tablecloth of black oilcloth out of a large tin box and covered the greasy inn table.

Over this we spread a white tablecloth, and from the same box produced napkins, plates, cups, knives, and forks, a can of jam and another of condensed milk, a little bag of sugar and a parcel of salt. By the time all the preparations were completed our dinner was ready. We ate and were refreshed and ready for our work.

The helper announced that the women were ready to receive me in their homes and that the men would call at the inn that evening. I took the cart, and accompanied by the helper, went out. The little town has wide and clean-looking streets. After a short run I came to the gate and entered to find the women who waited my coming. I suppose I am the first foreign lady the inhabitants of this quiet city had seen, yet they received me quietly, as if such visitors came every day. The home is not unlike all other homes of the poor Chinese. The lady of the house had a babe of ten days, yet was up and about and naturally looking feeble and very far from well.

This woman has an interesting history. I had heard of her as a learned lady and was curious to see her. She is the only child of her father's first wife. He is a teacher and at one time was rich. He wanted a son but had only this girl. Her mother died, his fortunes changed and he moved several times, teaching in different places. All this time he kept his daughter's feet unbound and passed her for a boy, kept her in the various schools he taught, and taught her with the rest. She not only read, but wrote, and she wrote so well that now she writes mottoes and various characters for sale.

The Chinese have their own ideas of good writing and have great admiration and respect for excellent writing. When they talked to her of Jesus she said she would write, 'One Ruler, Jesus Saviour' in large characters, and wrote the same in small characters, which I brought away with me.

This interesting woman, her father, and stepmother are all interested, and all profess to believe. The father and his wife were taken on probation. The daughter and her husband both intended to be taken on probation, but during my visit I discovered that they had not taken down their paper god. On speaking of the matter and asking still more about it afterward, it came out that the husband was afraid it would injure his business to take down his gods. His wife was willing. We thought that the man might feel differently on further instruction. The ideas of a heathen, who hears for the first time, must have time in which to fall in line with Christian thought. It is not easy to give up in a day the superstitions that have ruled for ages.

This woman who had passed for a boy so many years was betrothed at twenty, and her feet were bound then. Of course it was impossible to make them small as the usual little feet. But they have a way of crowding the toes so as to wear a sharp-pointed and short shoe. Often girls who are expected to do hard work are allowed to let their feet grow larger than usual, but the shoe is shaped like the other ones, and the foot is bound and made pointed.

We returned from Nan Kung in a bad dust storm. Between here and Nan Kung is a place the Chinese call Sand River. It is a bed of a former river. Some say it is an abandoned bed of the oft-shifting Yellow River, while others give other theories as to what caused the sandy stretch. But all agreed that any water would be an improvement over its present condition. The wind was very high on the day of our return, and everywhere the dust was thick and obscured the sun; but when we arrived on this sandy river-bed the air was as thick as during the most violent snowstorm, and each succeeding gust hid from view all objects much beyond the heads of the animals drawing our carts. Of course this dust covered our clothes, grated between our teeth, penetrated our hair, inflamed our eyes, and rendered itself generally disagreeable. The wind blew day before yesterday and today also, giving us one of its usual three days' blows of North China."

I took a cart and, accompanied by both Mrs. Lis, went to visit church members about two miles distant. The way people drop everything to follow and watch us, and seem to take little account of time; the freedom with which they crowd into each other's homes all make the various scenes in Christ's life seem natural and easily understood as they cannot be to those familiar only with Western modes of life.

At the first house we visited in this village we found old Mrs. Li and her husband. The narrow passage, the court inside, the mud walls, and the little rooms were all swept as clean as hard-packed earth can be swept. Children, great and small, and men and women immediately crowded every possible bit of standing room. The crowd was respectful enough, but so evidently came to see and hear in the same spirit that small boys run after a circus that it was almost useless to talk of the message I came to bear. Indeed, as I walk the streets of some of these villages, and see great and small scurrying from all directions, running ahead and then pausing to let me pass while they get a good look, as I hear the call passed from one to another and the hurry of feet behind, before and all around, as I see and feel all this, I am often reminded of the chorus,

The elephant now goes round,
The band begins to play.

I have been amused to notice that the expression with which some watch my movements and listen to my words is identical with the expression I have seen on faces intent on the antics of a monkey. At this home of Mrs. Li, I was importuned to talk each time I ceased, but it was with the same air that one might poke a bear at a menagerie, and the same air of satisfied amusement passed around as I began. Of course all there is left to do is to give the message with prayer, and trust the words may find an earnest soul among the many careless. "The crowd made satisfactory visiting impossible. This daily meeting with and addressing crowds, the strain of longing as set against a doubt that such minds can receive the light, tries the whole nervous system and leaves me tingling and exhausted. I am glad to find a day for more quiet work.

I am in a room about twenty feet by ten—my bedroom while at An Chia Chuang, four hundred miles from Peking. Overhead are beams supporting a tiled roof, all blackened by smoke of many years; underneath is an earthen floor. The windows are paper, a rude door is fastened by a movable wooden bar. On a rude couch is spread my little travelling mattress, a heap of boxes, water jars belonging to a native preacher's family, a table, and the bench on which I sit, the whole lighted by a candle brought all the way from Peking—and you have my surroundings. In the midst thereof I undertake to enlarge on my notes, taken by the way, and prepare a few pages that may interest my friends, who may be interested in me and my work—the Master's servant and the Master's work, I trust.

Just here my door is pushed open, and the dim light shows an old woman, followed by a younger one who carries a baby in her arms, and in turn is followed by several children. 'You are here,' the old woman says. 'Read what you are writing, and we shall hear.'

I must stop writing and talk to the people. This is a fair sample of the thousand and one interruptions every day is subject to. These women are picking at the lace at my wrists, remarking about my age, and asking all manner of questions as I write. After much talk with the women, and prayers with a company of church members and others in chapel, I am again by myself, excepting that Mrs. Lowry sits on my trunk at the other side of the table. She came in here to escape the odour of garlic and

71

onions that completely fills the other room.

This, my first day so far from home, has left me tired in a peculiar way. The Chinese women and girls pitch their voices in a very harsh key, and the language itself is not musical. After entertaining the constant stream of visitors for a few hours, the nerves tingle with every new footstep and quiver in expectation of the high grating voice very certain to follow. I bowed my head more than once today to ask for staying strength and patience to talk on while listeners were at hand. Poor creatures! They were quiet and respectful, much more so than usual; but they have no idea that the foreign maiden can have any objection to being gazed at, or to answering their idle questions.

There is absolutely no place where I can be alone unless I put the people out. They come into my room unless the door is locked, and seem to be conscious of no impropriety. I am reminded of an odd remark made by an itinerating missionary that the kingdom of heaven *does* come by observation in China.

Night. Have just come to my room to retire. The moaning, monotonous cry of a child in some near court reaches me here. I ask Mrs. Wang who it is that cries and why? She says: 'Oh, that is a hungry child. They are terribly poor, and the child continually cries for something to eat.' She adds that as she had no money to give them, she had taken a garment belonging to her second daughter and given it to this little one's mother. I sent Mrs. Wang to the kitchen for two bread cakes, purchased for my use, to give to the child. She has given them, and now the little one's moans are hushed. Poor little one not yet three years old! Poverty and suffering everywhere! These poor people seem so used to it that they mention, apparently without emotion, the most trying cases of dreadful slow torture of poverty and want.

CHAPTER 10

Marriage

In October, 1881, the Rev. Frank D. Gamewell arrived in Peking, which was an event destined to affect powerfully the career of Miss Porter. In the light of subsequent events it is evident that Mr. Gamewell was predestined to do a special work at a critical period in the history of the kingdom of God in China. Certain it is that his eventful life, which seemed at times to be the result of thoughtless chance, without purpose or significance, proved to be a plan of God preparing him to meet a fateful hour in the unfolding of his own great purpose.

He was the son of John N. Gamewell, the inventor of the Gamewell Fire Alarm and Police Telegraph. His family was closely identified with the Methodist Episcopal Church, South, his grandfather, two of his father's brothers and others of his kin being in the ministry of that church. His father's sister was the wife of Dr. Charles Taylor, the first medical missionary of the Methodist Episcopal Church, South, in China.

Frank was born in the storm centre of the Southern Confederacy at a time when intense political passions were hurrying the country on to civil war. His early memories are those of that dreadful strife, in which he saw his native town of Camden, South Carolina, lurid with the camp fires of an invading hostile host.

At the close of the Civil War he went with his father's family to Hackensack, New Jersey, a suburb of New York where his father's business was located. He prepared for college at the local academy, and chose for his profession that of civil engineer. He matriculated in Rensselaer Polytechnic Institute of Troy, New York, and was well advanced in his studies when he was interrupted by a serious accident. Later, he resumed his course in Cornell University, but before he had finished was stricken with a severe and protracted illness which

73

prevented his graduation with his class. He then concluded that God must have some other work for him than that he had chosen; and went to Dickinson College, Carlisle, Pennsylvania, where he graduated in the liberal arts course in 1881.

His call to missionary work came to him near the close of his college career in terms that could not be mistaken; and he was not disobedient to the heavenly vision.

How his coming to Peking Mission may have affected Miss Porter at the time does not appear in any direct statement in her writings. In a journal, in 1882, she speaks of "the event of events that modifies all my inner life, and permeates all my meditations, thoughts, and plans." This event culminated on the evening of June 29, 1882, in the marriage of Miss Porter and Mr. Gamewell in Asbury Methodist Episcopal Church, Peking, the ceremony being performed by the Rev. George R. Davis, who several years before had married Miss Maria Brown, who was associated with Miss Porter in the organization of the Woman's work in North China. Although Mrs. Gamewell by her marriage ceased to be an appointed missionary of the Woman's Foreign Missionary Society, and her name disappeared from the pay roll, she continued in her regular work as before. At the ensuing Annual Meeting, her appointment was announced thus: "Woman's Training School and City Evangelistic Work, to be supplied by Mrs. F. D. Gamewell."

The relation of the Woman's Foreign Missionary Society to the Annual Meeting and the church had not been authoritatively settled, and was the subject of frequent discussion. All matters relating thereto had been directed by the varying opinions of the Bishops who had visited the field. Mrs. Gamewell set herself with determination to have the question definitely and finally settled by the supreme authority of the church.

When Bishop Merrill visited the Mission in 1883 he recognized the chaotic condition of the legal relation of the Women's work to that of the General Mission work, and expressed the hope that the next General Conference would settle it. Pending it, he made the following decision: "The Bishop decides (1) that the ladies of the Woman's Foreign Missionary Society are not members of the Annual Meeting; (2) that he has no jurisdiction over their work; (3) that he cannot appoint them to the respective departments of their work; (4) that the Annual Meeting cannot receive their reports." This decision caused considerable dissatisfaction, for it set aside a custom that had prevailed from the founding of the Mission. Nevertheless, the meeting appointed a committee to receive the women's reports and present them to the meeting.

The General Conference having been memorialized, enacted that:

All missionaries sent out by this Society shall labour under the direction of the particular Conferences or Missions of the church in which they may be severally employed. They shall be annually appointed by the president of the Conference or Mission, and shall be subject to the same rules of removal that govern the other missionaries.

Subsequently one of our presiding Bishops at Peking declared that under this law he could not appoint women to work who were not regular missionaries of the Woman's Society. Mrs. Gamewell contested the point with the Bishop, and directed his attention to the rule of the Woman's Society which states:

Lady missionaries in charge of work and all missionaries of the Woman's Foreign Missionary Society are appointed by the president of the Conference at the same time and in the same manner that the appointments of the Conference are made.

The Bishop gracefully acknowledged the strength of her contention, and calling her the constitutional lawyer of the Mission, rendered his decision accordingly.

In 1884, two years after his marriage, Mr. Gamewell was appointed Superintendent of the West China Mission, which had its centre in the city of Chungking in the province of Szechuan. The Mission was in its infancy, having been started in 1881.

It was a severe ordeal for Mrs. Gamewell to part with her friends in Peking, and to leave the work of which she was one of the organizers, and into which she had put twelve of the best years of her life, and in which she had hoped to toil till she was summoned to her reward. It was like repeating afresh the sacrifice she made when she abandoned her country and kindred in obedience to the call of God. But there was no murmuring. When the pillar of fire moved on, she arose and followed.

Many years later she wrote a description of her trip up the Yangtse, which was published in The Chautauquan, by the courtesy of which magazine we make the following extract:

CHAPTER 11

Up the Yangtse

The great mass of the Yangtse's yellow water met us in the arms of the blue Pacific Ocean, thirty miles from China's yet-out-of-sight coastline. It seemed very appropriate that a river, whose waters could make such an impression upon the great deep, should be called 'Son of the Ocean,' although the authorities say that this is not a correct translation of '*Yangtse*,' and that the name was derived from one of the provinces which the river drains. Our vessel steamed from the blue into the yellow water over a line clearly defined upon the quiet sea. After a few hours we sighted the coast and soon thereafter made our arrival at Shanghai. Shanghai is not upon the banks of the Yangtse, but twelve miles up the Wusung River, which is a mile wide where it empties into the Yangtse. Many of the ocean liners are too large for the Wusung, so passengers are transferred to tugs which carry them up the Wusung to Shanghai.

At Shanghai our party made preparations for a long journey, for we were bound for Chungking in Szechuan, which empire-province lies on the borders of Thibet.

To be sure, one thousand miles of the journey would be made in a luxurious river steamboat; but beyond that were weeks of journeying in native boats, when we should be dependent upon our own bedding and food supplies. Fish, meats, fruit, vegetables, butter, and milk in sealed cans, are imported in large quantities, and such supplies, as well as portable stoves and everything else needed by the traveller in the Orient, can be purchased at the large stores to be found in Shanghai and other foreign settlements in China.

The Yangtse River, whose current we were to stem, and whose

76

scenes we were to explore, winds its way three thousand miles from the mountains of Thibet, where it has its source at an elevation of nearly two thousand feet above the sea level, to the coast where the mighty river joins the mighty ocean. In its course it receives waters from tributaries which drain more than half of the provinces of the empire—an area of 548,000 square miles. Sea-going vessels land their cargoes at Nanking, two hundred miles from the coast; large steamboats carry cargo and passengers to Hankow, about six hundred miles up the river from Shanghai, whence they are carried in smaller steamboats four hundred miles further up stream to Ichang.

When one considers the situation as seen by the Chinese he cannot wonder that ever since the encroachments of the foreigner in China began, trouble has been making for themselves and for the ever-advancing people from the West. Years ago native junks had all the coast trade of China; they swarmed the waterways that traverse the great plain, that carry commerce almost to the gates of Peking and reach the rich cities lying south of the Yangtse. Steam has supplanted the junks, many of which have rotted on the river banks. No wonder their owners think they have good reason to throw missiles at approaching steamboats, or to join the mobs which so often assault the foreigner, whose success has wrought Chinese failure!

From Shanghai to Ichang by steamboat, our way lay across three provinces, and touched upon the borders of two others. Kiangsu, the province in which Shanghai and Soochow are situated, is a coast province. The Grand Canal flows through its entire length from north to south, and it has other canals and waterways. The city of Chinkiang lies at the entrance of the Grand Canal to the Yangtse. Near the city may be seen two is- lands, made picturesque and interesting by temples and pagodas, whose roofs of yellow or green porcelain tiles tell of their imperial ownership. Farther up the river we touched at Nanking, celebrated as a literary centre. It is considered one of the first places of learning in the empire. From Nanking our course bent southwest and brought us to Kiukiang, on the south bank of the river and in the Province of Kiangsi.

This province has an area greater than that of all New England. There is a celebrated spot among its beautiful hills where Chu Hsi, the great commentator of Confucius, lived in the twelfth century, and which is visited by many of the Chinese *literati*, who make pilgrimages to this ancient home of their revered teacher and philosopher.

At Kiukiang one may find most beautiful porcelain, some of which is peculiar to that region. Not far from Kiukiang are porcelain manufactories which were established in 1004, and the best porcelain of the country is procured there. Still steaming upstream, we arrive at Hankow, on the north bank, in the Hupei province, and possibly visit Wuchang, the city's twin sister on the south bank, which is the capital of the province. The river Han joins the flood of the Yangtse at Hankow. At times the melting snow causes the river to rise forty or fifty feet, and its increased volume greatly augments the force of the Yangtse's powerful current which is here a mile wide.

From Hankow our course bent southwest, and brought us to Yo Chou, where the Yangtse touches the northern boundary of Hunan Province. The people of this province are reputed to be turbulent and bold. Soldiers recruited from Hunan are known as 'Hunan Braves,' but this appellation does not indicate that any great honour is accorded those 'braves.' For in China, public opinion finds its ideals and highest ambitions in literature, philosophy, and civil office. The pomp and glory of war do not appeal to the Chinese mind. A cultivated Chinese gentleman once made the pertinent inquiry, 'Why is it not more superior to lead the world in art, literature, and philosophy, than to be known as a conqueror by force of arms ?' meaning, 'What is there in the glory of arms to appeal to the people, capable of high attainments in intellectual pursuits?'

Proceeding up the Yangtse to within forty miles of Ichang, one catches sight of the mountains whose wild waters, deep gorges, and magnificent views give decided change from the monotony of scenery which prevails below Hankow, where the country north and south of the river is comparatively flat. At Ichang, the head of steam navigation, we chartered a native boat for the trip up to Chungking, which lies beyond the gorges and the rapids six hundred miles farther up the stream. The boat was eighty feet long, with four passenger cabins, ten feet by eight, and a crew of forty-two men, including the captain and pilot.

The price fixed for the boat was about one hundred and sixty dollars, which sum was supposed to cover the food and wages of forty-two men for one month, to pay for extra men at the rapids, to provide large quantities of bamboo ropes to be used in pulling our boat over the rapids, and, besides, to give the captain his profits.

The first day from Ichang brought our boat into the gorges and the beginning of troubled and dangerous waters. Three propelling forces were provided for the boat. There was a great sail to catch the favouring breeze when the waters permitted sailing; there were heavy-handled, broad-bladed oars, hung on pivots on each side of the deck forward of the passenger cabin, and eight lusty men ready to stand at the same; and there were hundreds of feet of bamboo rope in massive coils, waiting the call of the 'trackers.' The pilot took charge of a forward rudder—a massive oar forty feet long, projecting thirty feet over the bow. A dip of this oar many times saved our boat from capsizing. Close by the pilot was a drum, which, beaten according to the order of the pilot, was to direct the trackers; they must find foothold on the cliffs that shadowed the swirling waters, and, with ropes often one fourth of a mile long, pull the boat over the rapids. Men in small boats were to watch where the sharp rocks near the banks might catch and sever the sagging ropes.

The vertical walls of some of the gorges rise a thousand feet from the water and seem to overhang the narrow stream which they inclose. Through these gorges the wind fairly howls at times; then the boats wait for it to subside before they can sail through. If there be no wind, the oars are brought into requisition. Beyond the gorges, the towpath sometimes leads several hundred feet above the river, along precipitous mountains, and across the face of cliffs, where there appears to be hardly foothold for a goat. At each rapid, there is a little settlement of trackers, who are employed to aid each boat crew in passing the rapids. Often as many as one hundred extra men are needed for each boat. The boats tie up or anchor below the rapids and wait their turn. It sometimes happens that the boats are so numerous that the last comers have to wait several days for their turn.

Contrasted with the monotony we had experienced on the lower Yangtse, we had interest and excitement enough when our turn came to be pulled over the rapids of the upper Yangtse. Long tow-lines were thrown to the trackers. The drum signalled and the boat swung into the current. Then we saw the

WIND-BOX GORGE—YANGTSE RIVER

men bending almost to the ground, as they tugged at the long ropes, but the boat moved so slowly against the rushing, roaring waters, that it seemed not to move at all. At last, after a half hour of tugging trackers, roaring waters, rolling drum, and shouting pilot, our boat passed the two or three hundred yards of rapids, and swung into calmer waters, to repeat the experience at each one of the series of rapids which infest the waters of the upper Yangtse.

For two weeks our course lay over turbulent waters, through narrow gorges, under frowning precipices, and in the shadow of lofty mountains. A member of our party remarked that she felt oppressed by the continual grandeur of it all—as though she were passing through Hades.

As we neared Chungking the mountains receded somewhat, and a more restful hill country filled the foreground. One day, a month after we left Ichang, we swung around a bend of the river in sight of the city. The vast and solemn solitudes out of which we had come left us with an impression of having arrived at the end of the world, with the habitations of men left far behind, and the great city, with its frowning wall encircling the rocky spur on which the city lay, seemed an unreal thing, a vision.

CHAPTER 12

Chungking

Chungking is a city of about two hundred thousand inhabitants, situated on a bluff three hundred feet above the Yangtse and the Chialing, a tributary from the north, commanding in clear weather a magnificent view of the southern hills. But if the Chinese have a love for Nature, their mode of life in this city would not reveal it. The best properties are inclosed in high walls which completely shut out the view. However excellent these so-called compounds may be for purposes of protection from the madding crowd, they shut one in from the sweet sunshine and God's free air.

Such a property had been purchased by our Mission. Imagine four plastered mud walls rising above the roofs of the houses, pierced by two gates, one on the south, opening on the main street, and the other on the north, opening on a lane terraced above the city which clung to the steeps below. Within this inclosure were Chinese buildings two stories high, built a few feet from the wall around the quadrangle, and fronting on the open court within. This court was a rectangle twenty-five by thirty-five feet. It was overhung on all sides by the projecting roofs of the houses, wet with rain or soaking mists, dripping with dampness like the stones of a well. Day was far advanced before the morning sun could touch the pavement of the court, and at times by three o'clock in the afternoon it was necessary to light the evening lamps. Ghosts of rheumatism and pneumonia clad in garments of steeping moisture walked defiant in this sloppy cavern.

The houses of the Mission were so close as to be practically one building, in which privacy was impossible for those whose senses were keen. In one of these buildings was an orphanage, from which the moans and cries of Chinese children were heard through the livelong night, and never ceased in the so-called light of day.

Until one had accustomed himself to these conditions he found it all but impossible to breathe or think. Let him go to the northern gate to inhale the breath from the river and the hills, he might possibly be startled by the corpse of a baby falling inward with the opening door. That was not an unusual occurrence. Wretched parents would adopt this dreadful method to secure the burial of their dead, for the law required those on whose premises a corpse was found to give it burial. More frequently on opening the door, a living babe would fall in. In these instances it was always a girl, and usually one that was sickly or possibly, deformed. After a few such uncanny experiences one would rarely open that gate for refreshment.

Such was the home into which Mr. and Mrs. Gamewell entered on December 14, 1884. In the Mission of Chungking at that time were six missionaries: the Rev. and Mrs. Spencer Lewis, Dr. and Mrs. G. B. Crews, and two representatives of the Woman's Foreign Missionary Society, Miss Gertrude Howe and Miss Frances Wheeler. Little did they dream how soon and by what tragic means that heroic company was to be scattered abroad.

Mrs. Gamewell writes of her home thus:

Our West China Mission has its present home in a 'well,' or a series of wells. The buildings which unite to form these wells are fine buildings; they are well built; they are supported by many expensive pillars of wood; they are handsomely orna- mented with elaborate carving. But our fine houses, with only a 'well' for a yard, seemed a prison; we pined for the free, pure air, a broader sky, and more light; so our thoughts turned toward breezy Ko Lo Shan and its ruined temple.

There is not much pure air to be had in the city or in any near neighbourhood of the city. This is a coal-producing country. Soft coal abounds, and is the fuel in common use. This fact, by the way, introduces a feature into the landscape of this country not often observed in the North, namely, chimneys. A mixture of clay and coal dust, which gives off more gas than smoke, is used extensively in the North, and the natives manage to dis- pense with chimneys, as they could not if they used this smoke- producing bituminous coal.

A cloud of drifting smoke hovers over Chungking just as a heav- ier cloud hangs over Pittsburg. The smoke, added to the haze or fog, which enshrouds this province for at least six months of the twelve, makes the dirty streets and narrow courts of the city very gloomy. But the inhabitants seem to rise superior to their surroundings, or to be oblivious of all things disagreeable. They carry contented countenances, and are much given to feasting. They seem a cheerful people, careless of all things spiritual, and have a ready faculty of putting away or disregarding entirely all serious subjects. Women come in large numbers to the chapel, but the cheerful reason which they so cheerfully give, always is that they come for amusement.

After careful consideration it was decided to tear down a portion of the Chinese buildings and with the material erect a chapel elsewhere, thus not only improving the condition in the compound, but also facilitating evangelistic work among the natives. A property also was selected and purchased on the great road to the capital of the province and the principal cities of Szechuan, about three miles from the city mission, and beautifully situated on the high bank of the river. Here it was proposed to erect a hospital, a girls' school, and mission homes. Building was begun in March, 1886, and it was confidently expected that by December of that year the work would be practically finished. With this change not only would the missionaries be more agreeably located, but the opportunities for mission work would be greatly enhanced, for on this road great multitudes were constantly passing to and fro who were ready to pause for a few moments to see and hear the foreigners with their new doctrine.

The prospect for large usefulness was very cheering. While the people did not want the gospel, they certainly were in great need of it. Nor was it difficult to get the ear of the common people. Were it not for the *literati* and the official classes, who were constantly appealing to their superstitions and passions, the poor and distressed could have been readily reached. As elsewhere, the hospital with its beneficent work would win the respect and love of a people who certainly were not void of the human sentiment of gratitude. And the school was steadily disproving the absurd and popular superstitions concerning the "foreign devils," or "ocean demons," as the words mean.

The little band of missionaries was anticipating with great hopefulness their entrance upon their new quarters with its enlarged facilities for their work. Mrs. Gamewell's letters are bright with visions of great usefulness. The following are selections from a lengthy description of a day's trip she and others of the Mission made to the celebrated Ko Lo Mountain with its decaying temple:

Our chairs were ready. Across the narrow court loud voices were calling back and forth under the huge roof, which, supported by its tall black pillars, shades so many feet of our narrow quarters with cool shadows by summer and chill gloom by winter. The men who were to carry us uphill and downhill, and uphill again, and land us above the clouds, in a region of pure air, after much talking and running to and fro, finally adjusted their shoulders to their respective burdens, and turned their sandaled feet toward the only gate which opens from the landward side of the city.

Issuing from the city gate, the traveller has before him range after range of low hills, and higher hills stretching away as far as the eye can follow, until they are lost in a background of lofty peaks, sharply defined against the sky. The roads are paved with slabs of stone, and where the natural rock comes to the surface, it is cut flat and made to do duty in place of the usual slabs of stone. Over the steep places the stones are cut or laid in steps, and it is not uncommon to find a hundred or more of these steps in one ascent.

The valleys and hillsides are dotted all over with white farmhouses, which look clean and pretty at a distance, but are dirty and unsightly when seen near at hand. The farmers of Szechuan do not live in villages, as do the country people of the North, but in separate houses apart from each other, each farmer in the midst of his fields. Perhaps the general habit of living apart may account for the more peaceful temper of Szechuan people, as compared with the villagers of the North.

Their whitewashed houses, in the midst of bamboo groves or the vivid evergreens, are very inviting when seen from a proper distance, while the mad villages of the North, whether seen near at hand or afar off, are never inviting.

Some distance below the temple a heavy stone wall encircles the peaks and incloses the temple and its spacious grounds. It was a gate in this wall at which we entered, and, ascending yet other steps, we came to the temple itself. The temple is fast going to ruin; it is full of gods, helpless to save themselves, their abode, or their votaries. The place is in charge of a reprobate and poverty-stricken old priest, who is thought to gloat over the falling of any part of the fast-decaying buildings, because he then can make a little money by selling the timbers and tiles.

At the same time he would not dare to tear down any building, however dilapidated its condition, for fear of the people.

A noble tree covers one building with its grateful shade. This tree is so large, and occupies so conspicuous a place, that it can be seen miles away. A forest of fine trees used to shade this mountain, but the forest has faded away under the stroke of avaricious hands, keen to make gain by selling the timber. Now only shrubs and small evergreen trees shade the mountain slopes.

We selected rooms under the big tree, to be repaired for a retreat from the scorching heat of the summer, ate our lunch, spread in the priest's room, feasted our eyes upon the far-reaching views to be had on every side of the mountain, and then hastened our return to the city, fifteen miles away. Back we came to our dull rooms and narrow courts, but with new vigour in the blood, new inspiration in the soul, and a renewed faith; a spirit born of the Creator of the mountains, the rivers, and the sky seemed to accompany us, and ever and anon, through the dull but busy days which followed, called to mind those words, suggestive at once of a beautiful day and of the help we have in God the giver: '*I will lift up mine eyes unto the hills, from whence cometh my help.*'

CHAPTER 13

Evil Omens

The glowing sunshine was soon to be obscured by a destructive storm. Ominous mutterings presaged a furious outbreak. The contemptuous cry, "Foreign devil!" had in it a murderous accent, and coarse men became bolder in their insults day by day. Men of the ruder sort seemed bent upon provoking the foreigner to some offensive act which might give occasion for assault. When a missionary was climbing up the stone steps of the streets of the mountain city, a great giant coolly threw himself down across the path, while the leering crowd yelled vile words. Occasionally our people would suffer something far more serious than insults and threats.

The following is from a journal written by Mrs. Gamewell while a prisoner with other foreign women in the *yamen* of the magistrate in the city of Chungking:

After months of delay and search and discouragement a beautiful place commanding a view of both rivers was purchased. It was purchased from different parties in parts and at different times, so that a month or more passed after the first portion was made ours before the purchase of the other parts was accomplished. All was made ours by January 30, 1886, and the deeds were stamped by the magistrate, and a fee paid for the stamp, a fee of four or five per cent on the purchase price. During all these negotiations and official transactions there was not one word of protest or hint of objection to our possessing the place either from people or the officials.

A month was allowed for tenants to move before work was begun. The Woman's Foreign Missionary Society had purchased the first piece and had obtained possession a month before our purchase was completed. They put up walls and a fence. Our place was walled in, and then the sites chosen and plans laid out for houses. Still not a word of objection. Booms were fitted up and Mrs. Crews and I went to live on the place. I came to the city each morning and back in the evening. Beautiful walk, healthful exercise! Work went on and we enjoyed our country homes and lived in expectation of enjoying our new houses.

On the 6th day of June Mr. Gamewell and Dr. and Mrs. Crews went to town to conduct services, and I remained for a quiet Sabbath of rest, and to have a foreigner on the place to see that the gate was kept closed and no material interfered with. Soon after noon some persons demanded admittance and were denied. Soon there began a clatter of stones on the tiled roof near the wall. The people outside were throwing. The throwing became violent, and I went out to see who was throwing, thinking that I might identify someone, and then Mr. Gamewell would enter a complaint.

Quite a little crowd was standing about the lowest of the three gates, the gate intended for a hospital gate. As I issued from the gate of the property of the Woman's Foreign Missionary Society, some were throwing and more were looking on. Before I came near enough to see who they were someone saw me and gave the word and they all ran away. I went in. The throwing was renewed. I went out again. The crowd, now larger, ran again. I stood by the hospital gate and one by one the crowd collected about me. I had in my hand a five-foot measuring pole of stout oak. As I stood and looked about, the people stood too, and seemed afraid of me. If I made a move in any direction, those who stood there took to their heels. I talked to the people.

They kept quiet and seemed interested, but said that they had come to see our place and wanted to come in. I asked if it was proper for a crowd of men to ask to visit a place when only a woman was there, or if they would let into their homes a crowd who threw stones and broke the tile roofing. I appealed in the best terms I knew to the 'li' (customs) of the Chinese, an appeal so often effective among Chinese. A few respectable people left. Indeed, the servants say all the first crowd left, and the final crowd was made up of lewd fellows of the baser sort who gathered afterward. However that may be, the crowd increased until there were approximately two hundred about the gate. The gatekeeper asked me to come out once more, and I went, staff in hand.

This 6th of June was the 5th of the Fifth Moon (a great Chinese feast day) and the day of the Chinese Dragon Festival. The people wanted to come in and were rude. One of the servants said: 'Wait until the place is finished and we will invite you in.' They replied: 'We are working people and cannot come any other day. We intend to come in today.' I told them that people who had no '*li*' (manners) and wanted to go contrary to their own customs were not to be trusted; they would be sure to take things from the place if let in.

It was now so late that I knew the gentlemen must be on their way from town, and I hoped to gain time so that they might arrive. But the people grew so rude that the servant who had asked me to come out to the crowd now begged me to go in. Our cook went for a chief of police. When he arrived the people only laughed at him, and he could not disperse them. When I started in, someone threw at me and the crowd set up a howl. I backed against a wall. The official and cook managed to keep the crowds back until I got away. While I stood outside the last time, a bright-faced little girl stood beside me, and when I started in she came out of the crowd and followed me back, talking in a trembling and yet sympathetic voice. She went on and asked if she might come to the house with me, and if I would teach her to write.

She chattered on so bright and cheery, a perfect little sunbeam shining through a dark cloud. I left the cook in the street, and, as it was almost supper time and the gentlemen would soon be home, I thought I would prepare supper. I heard a great pounding at the gate and feared they might get in. Remembering how they ran from me at first, I thought that with Mr. Gamewell's gun I might make them run again, in case they got in, and perhaps keep the place until the gentlemen came. They were expected now every minute. I put the gun together the best I could, and took it, unloaded of course, and went into the kitchen.

The little girl stood at the door and soon announced: 'They are in. They are coming.' Sure enough, they had broken down the immense hospital gate and were crowding in. I took the gun and started toward them. When a hundred or more feet away the crowd caught sight of the gun and made off in haste through the broken gate. I went down and stood guard at the gate while one half of the great door was shut and braced up with heavy stones. I saw there would be a struggle if we attempted to have the other half put up. So I stood guard keeping out the crowd, hoping for the return of the gentlemen.

At this juncture the cook went to Fu Tou Kuan for the magistrate. A man diverted my attention by coming up with a child and pretending to be a friend whom I did not recognize. Suddenly someone seized the barrel of the gun. The crowd sprung to his assistance, the servants to mine. Two servants and I pulled one way and as many as could get hold of the barrel pulled the other way. As I pulled in desperation what thoughts crowded my mind! 'Frank's gun, a gift from his brother, now dead. Just arrived, not yet used. How silly to bring it out! What shall I do if they get away with it ?' How we pulled! We had an advantage in having hold of the butt end. They threw at me and pounded my fingers with their fists, while others pulled. There could be only one end. They made off with the gun, and I stood in distress and shame to see it go.

The stampede for the gun seemed to frighten those outside, and the crowd gave away and many ran right away. There was hubbub about me. One said they did not believe in tobacco, and I turned to see the servants looking at me in great concern. The old gateman had some fine tobacco in his hand which he offered to tie about my finger. Then I saw that the index finger of my right hand was cut almost to the bone. The blood had flowed quite a little stream, staining the soft stone quite red. My dress was spattered with mud, my hair and neck on one side were all plastered with mud, and on the same side a big swelling was rapidly rising just below the temple. The crowd had caught sight of me and fled in dismay, afraid of being held accountable, no doubt, for a worse task than they attempted to undertake.

Just here the cook came in and said the official *Pu-kuan* would not attend to the affair. I sat down in the gate alone, and for a second hot tears flowed from grief for the lost gun. Then the servants came, and directing them to put up the other half of the gate, I hastened to make myself tidy before Mr. Gamewell should get back. I dressed my finger, and washed the mud off, and had only time to hurry into my ulster and a tie, when the official from Fu Tou Kuan walked in.

Probably hearing of a bigger disturbance than he had thought possible, he came in to forestall disastrous consequences to himself in case anyone should be called into account for the disturbance of the day. He said he would get the gun for me and went away. He met the crowd venturing in again and put them out, though the servants said his manner was as if ridiculing foreigners at the same time he was putting the men out of the gate.

Soon after the official was gone Mr. Gamewell came in. A man had gone to town to call him, and met him at the corner of the city on his way out. In great anxiety he came on. He sat down and only looked and looked at me after I showed him that I was not seriously hurt. He suffered more than I did. I did not even know that I was hurt, until all was over. I did not know when I was hurt. Probably the trigger tore my finger, but I did not feel it. By and by the doctor came in. He had heard alarming reports on the road and came in looking pale. He dressed my finger most scientifically, using carbolic acid, which benumbed the finger and prevented any pain.

CHAPTER 14

Chungking Riot

The Chinese have an instinctive antipathy for foreigners. Every attempt to explain it by rehearsing the immediate occasion of its expression is superficial and unsatisfactory. It is probably the evolutionary product of what has been called "the geologic ages of their national history." In their millenniums of isolation they have developed ideals of their own, unimpaired by close contact with those of other nations, till the people have come to look upon them as the final good, beyond which there could be no better.

Their ideals and ours are not only different, but really antipodal. This is the order in which they grade men: beginning at the highest is the emperor, the representative of heaven; next below him is the scholar, who alone is qualified to rule; then comes the farmer; after him the mechanic; still lower, the trader; and at the bottom of the social scale, the soldier. With this ideal in mind we can imagine how the deepest instincts of the Chinaman must have been shocked by his first contact with the Western world. When the white-faced foreigner came to him in the representatives of the East India Company it was for trade. Then came the soldiers who with terrible slaughter fought their way to the very gates of the imperial city. Following these lowest orders, came mechanics, erecting strange buildings and constructing railroads which defaced the country and threatened native labour. And in nearly every instance the presence of the foreigner meant the extension of the opium curse, the loss of valuable territory, and the humiliation of their rulers.

It would be too much for us to expect the average Chinaman to distinguish between the foreigner and the Christian. To him all foreigners are Christians. Besides, his idea of a Christian is largely that created in his mind by the Roman Catholic Church, which came to that country in 1246, and after more than a century of propaganda, was lost in Mohammedanism and Buddhism, only to return again in 1582, from which time it has continued till the present hour, having nearly seven hundred thousand communicants. If the church had confined itself to spiritual matters, the results might have been different; but it has been true to its traditions, and has meddled in civil affairs to such a degree as that a bishop assumes the rank of a Chinese governor, and moves among the people with all the showy splendour of a civil officer. The result is that the jealousy of the officials is irritated, and the antipathy of the people, more especially the student class which aspires to office, is excited to the point of murderous hatred.

This instinctive hostility to the foreigner becomes almost a religious frenzy among the unreasoning masses, when it is fired by popular superstitions. The foreigner erects buildings above a given elevation, and thus obstructs the flight of irritable spirits and excites their rage against a helpless people. The baptism of dying infants is a part of a devilish science by which certain parts of the human body may be put to the transmutation of metals. The erection of orphanages is for this same fiendish alchemy. Missionaries hang no streamers on the trees of Szechuan in order to placate the spirits that are there. They spill no blood of a cock on the prow of their boats when they start on a voyage. They want little Chinese children so as to tear out their eyes and use them for medicine. Thus superstitions, which are sure to become dominant when vital religion disappears, have made this people as inflammable as tinder, when fired by the student and official classes.

For these general reasons riots were of frequent occurrence throughout the empire. One never could tell when the volcano on which he was living would shake with wrath and pour out the hissing flames of mob fury. The most trifling incident might prove the occasion of a most terrific explosion. Such an outbreak occurred in Chungking in July, 1886. Mr. Gamewell names as the immediate occasion of this irruption the presence of a large body of military students during examinations, the high price of rice and the consequent suffering among the poor, rendering it easy for the students to incite the people to violence in hope of plunder, and the inactivity of the officials who, if they did not help the riot, at least did nothing to restrain it. Dr. Arthur H. Smith says that:

> The people of this remote province are not unfriendly to foreigners excepting when they are stirred up to opposition by

their officials. A foreign bureau at the capital of the province has been shown to be the active agent for the diffusion of anti-foreign virus over this entire region, to the incomputable loss of unnumbered persons. The rioters of 1886 openly declared that they had authority from the emperor and from the officials to extirpate Christianity.

If the purpose of the officials in exciting or favouring the popular tumult was to expel Christianity from their midst, they could not have acted in greater unwisdom. They started a cyclone which they could not control, black with swirling clouds of insane passion, full of uproar, deafened to every call of mercy or reason, increasing in power with every mad bound, whirling in its furious coils the wrecks of missions and consular agencies, but a power that was sure to stir the conscience of the entire Christian world, and rouse the governments of Christendom to force restitution and to open the way for the entrance and security of all who chose to enter the land. Mrs. Gamewell in the darkest moment of that riot with clear vision saw the outcome, and said: "They think thus to shut the door, but are really swinging it wide open."

The mad fury of a mob is far more to be dreaded than a cyclone. It is cruel, pitiless, fiendish. Every brutal passion, long held in leash, is let loose. Every noble feeling of the soul, even the restraining sentiment of fear, is lost in an unthinking impulsion. The muttering of a cyclone is music itself in comparison to the shrieks of an infuriated populace. One might as well reason with the tumultuous sea, or attempt to retain the thunderbolt in the cloud, as to resist this onrushing human cyclone.

This terror struck our little company in Chungking. They heard it from afar, and saw it bounding in frightful destruction from place to place. It swept away every trace of the foreigner wherever it struck. It paused not for a moment to attack even the British consular agency, which was the second property in the city destroyed. The Methodist compound was the last attacked. Its inmates could see the destructive work on the Roman Catholic cathedral which was not far away, and they knew that their turn would come next. There was no time for counsel. Mr. Gamewell hastily sent a man to secure a boat, hoping to escape to the river, on the treacherous current of which they might float away to where God might lead them.

But it was too late. The shrieking mob had gathered at the front gate which had been barricaded, and began to batter it down. The missionaries lifted their hearts to God in prayer. None of them were terror-stricken, for even then, as Mrs. Gamewell said, they realized the promise fulfilled, "*Lo I am with you alway, even unto the end of the world.*"

While the mob was forcing its way through the front gate of the mission premises an officer came to the rear gate and urged the missionaries to hasten for their lives. It seems that the magistrate, however much he may have sympathized with the purpose of the mob to rid the city of all traces of the foreigners, was very unwilling to have any of them slain. He was wise enough to foresee the consequences, and had planned to shelter them in his *yamen* until he could arrange for their safe conveyance down the river.

Everything the missionaries possessed, excepting what they carried on their persons, was swept away as by a conflagration. The following are selections from Mrs. Gamewell's journal written while a prisoner in the *yamen*. They were never revised for publication; but they reveal so perfectly the spirit of one in bondage for Christ's sake, that we dare not attempt any alteration. What they may lack of rhetorical finish is more than compensated in the spiritual atmosphere of one of the most significant periods in her personal history.

Toward the middle of the afternoon [July 2, 1886] we heard that Mr. and Mrs. Woods had gone to the magistrate's residence, and our servants urged us to go too. The gentlemen barricaded the gates and windows of the outside wall and sent for Misses Howe and Wheeler to come in. We could hear indistinctly the tumult of a mob about the Catholic cathedral. The gentlemen, that is, Dr. Crews and Mr. Gamewell (Mr. Lewis being over the river), went upstairs, and from there saw a mob chopping into the windows and raging around the place.

We thought we might escape to the riverbank or take a boat and drop down the river, but hesitated. In the meantime we sent for the men whom the magistrate said should guard our place. I procured a little box containing pins, cuff buttons and a specially treasured keepsake. As we talked in the court below suddenly a man rushed in excitedly and said the magistrate had sent for us to come to his *yamen*. We recognized him as the man who had come with credentials the day before. He had sedan chairs at the back gate. We had sometime before sent Miss Howe's four wards and Miss Wheeler's two wards with Sadie Crews to the carpenter for safe hiding, so there were five ladies, two gentlemen, and one little girl in our party.

Our chairs were hurried along by the back wall. The gentlemen were obliged to walk because the chairs were not sufficient. Dr. Crews took off his coat that the crowd might not have it to catch at. He shut his fist and strode along. Instead of being carried to the *yamen*, we were put dawn at a house which opened directly at the wall. It proved to be the home of a policeman. While here a note was sent to Mr. Lewis telling him of our situation, and a man dispatched with it. The man who guided us to this place presently was found missing. A crowd gathered and poured into our cramped quarters. The women of the house became uneasy and wanted us to go. The gatekeeper of the ladies of the Woman's Foreign Missionary Society came in and showed a package of silver about his waist. The carpenter also brought in his *cash* which served to pay chair hire. We saw they were already looting our homes, and we found that no distinction was made between us and the Catholics.

The crowd became very unpleasant, and just as we were beginning to feel uneasy our escort came in. He had a broken head and was spattered with blood. He said he had been down to the Catholic place. Likely he was, as his services as chief of police would be needed there; but it is also possible that he was off helping riot.

At first the crowd was disposed to block the way when we attempted to go out. This escort expedited our removal by shouting that he was to take us to the magistrate's *yamen*. As he shouted he pushed, and the crowd made way. One by one we elbowed our way to the chairs at the door. We had been there about an hour. Now we were carried off into the darkness, each alone in the closed chairs borne on the shoulders of men. My turn came and I took the seat in the chair, about which the crowd pressed closely, just as it was discovered that there were no more chairs. Mine was the last, and Mr. Gamewell was without a chair, and the turbulent city had to be crossed before we reached our destination.

I wanted to wait, but was borne off, and the last I saw or heard was Mr. Gamewell in the midst of a crowd who shouted boisterously for him to sit down, that it would not do for him to walk, etc. We were carried into the city and across some of the great streets through which men were carrying all manner of articles from foreign houses to Chinese houses, besides the furniture of natives who were moving out of the dangers of our neighbourhood; whether the furniture was from the looted homes of more unfortunate natives we could not tell.

Again we were carried through a gate which was not the *yamen* gate. The gate was deep and dark, and there was an order not to bring a light. We were hurried into a room which we learned was the home of the chief of police who was conducting our party. After a while we were asked to ascend a ladder and were stored away in a dark, windowless garret, and they asked us not to talk. Here we sat on the floor in a corner for the space of two or three hours, not daring to think what might have happened to Mr. Gamewell. But I prayed and seemed to receive the assurance of his safety.

Finally, word came that the magistrate had sent for us, and this time we were really to go to the *yamen*. An escort had come to conduct us. After a ride of several minutes we arrived at the *yamen*, and there found Mr. Gamewell where he had been carried directly after we left him. He had suffered anxiety for us, as he had expected to find us at the *yamen*, and doubted the truth of any account that was given of our whereabouts. Because of his urging, parties had been sent in different directions to find us. While in the garret some of our party saw the flames of the Catholic cathedral, which the mob burned after looting.

Mr. Gamewell met me in the *yamen* court only to say that we were in Chinese quarters and must conform to Chinese customs. So we shall be stored away in one court and the gentlemen in another. It was hard after a separation in the midst of danger to miss the joy of having the rest of the night in each other's company and together await developments. "Our party of ladies were led through a series of dimly lighted rooms into another, and there we found Mrs. Wood and Mrs. Copp and family. We had heard from the chief of police that the Nichols were in the keeping of another chief of police on the other side of the city.

Here we heard Mrs. Wood's and Mrs. Copp's story of how about thirty men took all the things out of Mr. Copp's house and made off, of how the ladies and children had fled to town, only to rest an hour or so when they had to fly from Mr. Wood's house before the approach of a mob, Mrs. Wood, with Mrs.

Copp's infant and Ruby, a bag of silver-forks, etc., and a sponge cake on a plate in her hand! She had only started when her chair was so torn that she left it and called a street chair. The chairmen carried her in her damaged chair to a chair shop, and there transferred her and her baggage to a street chair. They hurried swiftly away and landed Mrs. Wood, babies and baggage, in the *yamen* uninjured.

Mrs. Copp arrived without adventure. We were not long there when Mrs. Nichols came in. She had been through a hard siege. She was in the house with poor, sick Mr. McMullan when the mob burst through. They tore the silver pins out of her hair and searched her person for valuables. They pulled the bedding from under Mr. McMullan and tore the room to pieces in spite of their entreaties for mercy for the sick. They managed to carry Mr. McMullan away, finally, Mr. Nichols going with him to the policeman's house. Mrs. Nichols missed them and made for her teacher's (a friend) house.

A brutal man seized her by the collar of her dress and gave her a jerk forward and then a violent push backward which threw her on her face in the street. She got up and made off. Some teachers in the crowd said the man should not hurt her. The teacher class, however, had much to do with starting the mob, but they did not intend to take life. *They* are intelligent and know the serious consequences of such violence. Mrs. Nichols hid away in her teacher's house until a man came and took her to the policeman's house. The man carried her on his back through the crowd, and finally brought her with the rest of her party to the *yamen*.

We slept in our clothes and spent an uneasy night. Next day we heard that n wealthy Catholic named Lou had armed men and undertook to defend his home, though he had given up his shop to be looted. This Catholic is much hated. He held his own pluckily, and killed several men who came for plunder. The killing only excited the mob and made his case a desperate one should he fall into the hands of the mob.

The shedding of blood made the whale trouble take on a more desperate aspect. Mr. Bourne, the British resident, had been interested in our trouble from the beginning, and gave us much valuable assistance. It seems that the riot was anti-foreign without distinction in favour of anybody, with more violent demonstrations toward the much-hated Catholics. Mr. Bourne was to be no exception in the general attack. His house was attacked and he left it. He was on his way to the assistance of China Inland Mission, he writes, when the mob dragged the leader of his escort from his horse and injured Mr. Bourne himself. The magistrate was thrown down several times in the press about Mr. Bourne. The magistrate threw himself against Mr. Bourne's person, and declared that an injury to Mr. Bourne could only be made by first attacking himself, and so saved him from further violence.

Homeless and with resources gone, the only thing to do was to get down the river to the coast, send those whose condition made it necessary to the United States and take up the settlement of losses with the Chinese Government in Peking.

CHAPTER 15[1]

Down the Yangtse

July 13th, p. m. Now comes word that we *all* shall go tomorrow night. All day we have heard that all could not be planned for, and now the Tao Tai says all may go, and he will make out passports. Why this sudden change? We can only conjecture. Perhaps they have been waiting for some word from the capital, and it has come. But we cannot know. Read book of Daniel. God is good. He has drawn us very close to himself during these days of trial. Can we ever wander far again? 'Shall know how his love went before us each day, and wonder that ever my eyes turned away.'

July 14th, Wednesday. Last night came a letter from Mr. Bourne saying the Tao Tai (intendant of circuit) wanted a letter saying that 'as bills of losses had been received, the weather being warm, some of our party poorly, and nothing more to be done, we desire to go to Ichang,' and that he would have the letter written in Chinese and sent around for Mr. Gamewell to sign and send in, since Mr. Gamewell has no Chinese writer here. Then when the letter is received, the Tao Tai will send passports for our entire party. Now, this morning, they say we Americans are to start tomorrow morning and the English the next day. It rains, and perhaps a rain will delay our going. Well, we are in the care of Him who rules the rain and the great waters and overrules in the affairs of men. He can do all his will. And if it is his will, we shall be off tomorrow. If it is not his will, we are better off to be here. So we wait and pray and trust.

Whether the present situation is the result of strong active hostility on the part of the people at large, or is brought about by the direct work of the *literati* who hate foreigners, or by the rough military stu-

---

1. This chapter is composed of unfinished notes from Mrs. Gamewell's pen.

dents, or whether the officials have directed and stimulated known hatred to produce desired results, all this we cannot know. Any of these forces or all combined may have set us adrift without houses or goods or work. However the riot may have been stirred up it is certain the only object of the mob was to loot and get gain. At this time rice is very high, and the people are, many of them, desperate.

Night. The magistrate, insulting and threatening, said he was taking care of us, but in America they killed Chinese. . . . The magistrate says they have engaged two boats for us (the American party). Of course we do not know what to believe; but we know Whom we have believed.

Later, July 15th. Passports for Mr. Gamewell and myself, ladies, and girls have come, and, besides, word that the English are to go at the same time. Mr. Gamewell signed a paper like the one sent to the Tao Tai, but refused to add anything to it. It seems to have been accepted. Yesterday the magistrate told his wife to get black cloth to wrap our heads in to help disguise us, and we are to wear Chinese clothes. Today the magistrate says we are to leave in the third watch, and not in the daylight, as he first said.

This occasion brings out one of our number's wonderful capacity for emergencies. A simple faith seems to possess him, and his countenance shines confident and bright with the hope and courage and strength that is born of God. So for us, shut up where all depends upon God and there is no place for self-reliance, all self-depreciation and wavering disappears, and he is so steadfast and strong. Faith docs its perfect work, and he is capable of a very strong, pure faith. 'Bless the Lord, O my soul.'

After dinner. Boat papers for English and Americans all made out. Passports in except the first which was sent to the magistrate for Mr. Lewis and Dr. Crews on Monday. Hope runs high. We seem nearer going than at any other time.

Still 15th, 9:45 p. m. Just read an invitation to a feast to be eaten tonight before going to boat! Things all gone.

July 16th, 5:45 a. m. Up all night. Feast at one. To boats about two. Weighed anchor about 5 :45. Left in darkness. Lanterns swinging in the fog. Soldiers seen in the dim streets guarding our way down to the boat, soldiers and *yamen* runners guarding and pointing way. Magistrate came down and sat in his chair and exhorted the boat captains. So in the darkness we steal out of the city whose people have torn up every vestige of our home and left us with none of the treasure we brought with us two years ago.

On our boat, Misses Howe and Wheeler and five girls and ourselves. Other American boat, Mr. and Mrs. Lewis, and Nellie, Dr. and Mrs. Crews, and Sadie.

After keeping us in his *yamen* for two weeks the magistrate sent us at two o'clock in the morning of a summer day on board a boat, and with a strong guard saw us off on our perilous journey. Our return trip to the coast was made in a season when only extraordinary pressure would induce one to venture on the waters of the upper Yangtse The autumn and winter months are considered the safe season for navigating the river above Ichang. When the snows on the mountains begin to melt the water pours into the narrow channel of the river in great floods, rising sometimes in a few minutes sixty feet above its ordinary level.

Boats cannot travel at night and then tie to the banks or cliffs. There have been boats so tied which have been swamped by the descent of a wall of water, which came rushing through the darkness so swiftly that the boatmen had only time to hear the roar of the onrushing terror before it was upon them, and their boats, tied fast, went down. There are other dangers that make the navigation of the upper Yangtse very perilous. What in low water are rapids, in high water are whirlpools so numerous and powerful that boats cannot escape them.

When we left Chungking the floods were coming, and the season was at hand when the boatmen would refuse to risk their boats upon the waters. As it was, we were put upon a freight boat because the deck where we were to bestow ourselves was several feet below the level of the deck of a passenger boat; therefore, our weight would not make the boat so top-heavy and we would be in less danger of capsizing. Running away from threatening death, Death seemed chasing all about us. I knelt on our deck and so brought my eyes on a level with the deck in front, where our men were standing to the oars.

I could see shallow currents running on top of other currents and the water seemed to be going in every direction at once. Then came whirling the great black depths of the whirlpools! It was brave work our gallant oarsmen did. Standing face to the prow they rowed, the wind slapping about them and howling wildly. With great skill and precision they bent, might and main, to the oars. For an instant's relaxation, each man sat on the great beam-handle of his oar; then with a spring, every muscle in action, they bent again to the oars just in time to save us from disaster.

So we went through the whole day. Our hearts glowed with admiration and clove to those sturdy men of brawn and wondrous skill and courage on whose skill and faithfulness our lives depended. My face was quite near the feet of one of the two hindermost men. I watched their rhythmic tread as they kept step with the regular pat, pat of all the other feet. After a while the man, looking over his shoulder, shouted above the howling wind and asked: 'Are you afraid?' I shouted back: 'With such men as you at the oars, how could I be afraid ?' Simple-hearted as he was, brave and skilful, his face broke into a broad smile, and he shouted my reply to the man in front of him, and he in turn shouted it to the next, and he in turn shouted it to the next, until the word had gone the rounds of the whole lot. Each man as he heard it beamed upon me with a smile of good will, which good will was manifested all the rest of the way down the river. Such is the power of a word of appreciation and so akin to all mankind are those brave boatmen of the upper Yangtse.

These men on the boats of the upper Yangtse are the only picturesque Chinese whom I have seen. To begin with, they have no queue in sight. The queue is wound around the head and covered with a turban. Many of the boatmen are from Hunan, that province of the turbulent and bold and brave. The queue was imposed upon the Chinese as a sign of their subjugation, when the Manchus overthrew the government less than three hundred years ago. These men of the upper Yangtse have never been reconciled to the queue. They dare not cut it off, for that would be treason to the government, and their heads also might be cut off. So they hide the queue under a turban, and the effect is very pleasant. They bind their legs from ankle to knee with long bandages to save from strain, or rupture of blood vessels, in hard climbing. Their trousers end at the top of the band-ges, and they wear sandals woven of straw upon their feet. The combination, finished with short jacket girded tight with a sash, is picturesque and attractive.

Our men brought us from Chungking to Ichang in four days. We had taken just four weeks for the journey upstream from Ichang to Chungking. The difference speaks volumes concerning the currents on which we rushed to our destination.

Doubtless the boatmen are still urging their skilful way over the waters of the upper Yangtse. But mighty changes are developing rapidly all along the lower reaches of the river and pushing surely and permanently into the innermost parts of the great empire.

On reaching Shanghai Mrs. Gamewell returned to the United States on account of her health, and Mr. Gamewell spent the winter in Peking in the settlement of losses incurred in the Chungking riot.

CHAPTER 16

Asbury Church, Peking

After Mr. Gamewell had settled with the imperial government the claim for indemnity for our mission property, he returned to the United States, and later was reappointed to Peking. It was a great joy both for Mr. and Mrs. Gamewell to be back in their old field. He was assigned a place in the university and she fell naturally into the old lines of work to which she had given many years of her life. She was given special charge of the training school, the object of which was to drill in Bible doctrine and methods of work women who had been carefully selected from church members throughout the Conference. These women, when trained, would return to their homes and become most efficient forces in the work of the local churches. Among them there arose many veritable "mothers in Israel," like Mrs. Wang, whose sterling character and energetic work remind us of those women who were such effective forces in the early history of American Methodism.

Thus many years passed for Mrs. Gamewell in quiet routine of daily duty, unbroken by any startling occurrence. She slept and rose night and day, and the seed sprang and grew up, she knew not how: the blade, the ear, the full corn in the ear. In addition to her training school there were two things in which she took a very active part and on which she put the stamp of her own individuality. One was the erection of the large and beautiful Asbury Church. Dr. Lowry, after her decease, wrote: "Her letters more than anything else made possible Asbury Church in Peking, with all it means in the life and work of the mission." The story is fully told in one of her letters of appeal to Chaplain McCabe, then corresponding secretary of the Missionary Society of the Methodist Episcopal Church. The substance of this letter is here given:

We are in trouble. Let me tell you our trouble, and please help us. The Mission chapel is giving way. We began to prop and mend it a year ago, but now the walls lean worse, the cracks are wider, and the timbers bend more threateningly. If you could stand by the old weather-beaten chapel and hear its history, so interwoven with all the Mission's joys and sorrows, and its hopes, past and future, and realize how much depends upon our Mission chapel, your voice would ring out with energy of speech and song that would win for us the help we need. It is no shame for the chapel to fall.

It has stood nearly twenty years and cost only two thousand dollars when it was built. We knew it could not be long-lived because there was not money enough to build substantially. It is now the oldest building in the Mission. Dr. Pilcher, then only three years in the field, superintended the building. The inclosed is a photograph of the interior, showing the casket in which Dr. Pilcher's remains were buried and the decorations at the time of the funeral. Within a month of Dr. Pilcher's death (November, 1893) the chapel was discovered to be tottering to a fall.

Dr. Pilcher was superintendent of our afternoon Sunday school. This Sunday school began as a class of the Mission's Sunday school. The class developed into two classes, one for girls and one for boys. These classes grew so large that they alone filled the chapel. The Sunday school had to be held in two sessions, one in the morning for Christians and one in the afternoon for the boys and girls of the neighbourhood. The young men and women of our Mission schools are the teachers in this after-noon school. The school serves as a training-school for them as well as a means of reaching street children with the gospel.

The chapel has seating capacity for four hundred, but often five hundred are present at the afternoon Sunday school. Some sit on the altar steps, and some are held on the knees of others, and some stand up. Many of the children come shivering in rags from forlorn homes, in comparison with which the chapel is a paradise of warmth and good cheer. The Sunday school hour is the one bright spot in each seven days for such. The children wait eagerly for each returning Sabbath. They shout as we pass on the street: 'How many days to next Sunday?'

They gather in increasing crowds about our gates from noon

Sunday until the bell rings and the gates are opened at three. These are the children who once ran in terror at sight of us, feared our 'evil eyes,' believed we used children's eyes for medicine, and whose first stages of recovery from terror were marked only by bad names called from safe distances. The whole neighbourhood has been reformed in the matter of reviling by the influence of our Sunday school.

The children were induced to come to us, in spite of fears and prejudices, by giving picture cards, one to each child who should come. The interest is so sincere now that most of the pupils would come if there were no picture cards given, but we prefer to continue giving cards because bright cards once a week are great treasures to children who have so little. I know some pinched- faced little folks exchange their cards for something to eat. One cold day I saw a child not more than six years of age hand her card to a peddler and receive in its place a cup of hot soup. The eagerness of the child would make any heart ache.

Now this Sunday school is the only one of such size and such intense interest in China. Visitors always exclaim: 'I have seen nothing like it in China!' The school has been in existence as a school only one year and a half. It is the rich fruit of years of toil and waiting. Do you understand what it would mean to shut our gates for weeks and months with no promise as to the near future? Suspicion would follow disappointment, and the Chinese would think we had ceased to want them in our chapel, reasoning in the same way as when, believing all missionaries to be doctors, they think we do not cure their diseases because we do not want to. Work so slowly accumulated would disintegrate before our eyes and we powerless to help.

Besides the Sunday schools, every other department of our Peking work depends in a measure upon the chapel. The university students meet in the chapel for morning prayers. Preaching services and prayer meetings depend upon the chapel. The chapel is the only assembly room for funerals and weddings. Christmas is celebrated in the chapel. There is no place for commencement exercises but in the chapel. Annual Meetings have no accommodations outside the chapel. What will become of these interests when the chapel falls? When the chapel was built its size seemed so out of proportion to the numbers assembled and the work then under way that our friends remarked: 'You must have great faith to build so large a house with any hope of filling it.'

The faith has been rewarded. The work has so outgrown the chapel accommodations that for several years the Mission has felt the need of a large church, but schools and country work have been in such urgent strait, and we need such a big church next time one is built, that the Mission has delayed asking for an appropriation for a church, hoping that the time might come when they could ask with a hope of receiving it, about ten thousand dollars, to build a church that would answer Mission purposes for the next twenty years.

If you find it in your power to help us to a new church, you will be sending a broad beam of cheer into the shadows, that will lift us up and strengthen us to a degree that perhaps you little imagine.

The appeal was successful. Mr. and Mrs. Gamewell came to America and devoted much of their time to this work. He studied plans with the aid of a competent architect, and decided on the erection of a building which should be made chiefly of brick and wood, and which should accommodate fifteen hundred persons. He returned to Peking and superintended the erection of the church. It was when finished not only the most conspicuous architectural feature of the Methodist compound and the centre of its life, but also the largest Protestant ecclesiastical structure in China.

CHAPTER 17

Peking Sunday School

Mrs. Gamewell was greatly interested in the Sunday school and devoted much of her time and strength to it. The following is taken from one of her published leaflets:

"At the time of the building of the first Methodist church in Peking friends of the missions remarked, 'You must have large faith if you expect to fill so large a church in your day.' Only a few years passed and a Sunday school of four hundred filled every seat. Every Sunday workers whose hands were full of all sorts of work during the week united in the work of the Sunday school, and the Sunday school early became the chief joy of the Mission.

At first the students from the Mission schools and the Christians and servants of the Mission were the only pupils, but after a while a few children of the neighbourhood ventured in. The children had heard their elders call the missionaries 'foreign devils,' and they had been told that foreign devils used children's hearts and eyes to make medicines, so, of course, they were slow to venture within the courts of the foreigner.

A recruit from New England, Miss Cushman, joined the Mission, and she brought with her a talent for bringing things to pass and a quantity of picture cards. The cards were such as every business house used to issue, combining an advertisement and a beautiful picture on each card. She took charge of the class of street children, and she gave to each child a card and promised to give a card to every little girl who should join her class in Sunday school. The cards proved very attractive; then, besides, other children could see for themselves that the first children to attend Sunday school had not lost their hearts or eyes.

They ventured in, in constantly increasing numbers, until at last the class was too large to meet with the rest of the Sunday school. It had to have a room all to itself. Then that room was soon filled to overflowing. The children sat on the seats and on the backs of the seats; they sat on each other's laps; they sat on the floor; they sat on the table and under the table. Indeed, the teacher had to take her place before the children should come in, and when they were all there she had just standing room and no more. And when visitors called the teacher could not move an inch to receive them and they could only look through the door, inside of which there was no room for them, and pass on exclaiming: 'Wonderful! wonderful!'

Finally, the Mission determined to make a whole Sunday school of this one class, and it was done. In the morning was the regular Sunday school, with Christian members and students from the mission schools as pupils, and the missionaries as teachers. In the afternoon the children of the neighbourhood and any adults who cared to come, were the pupils in another Sunday school and the pupils from the morning Sunday school were the teachers. The afternoon Sunday school became a training school, where the Christian students were brought into contact with those who knew not God and practiced the art of winning them for the Saviour already so dear to their own hearts.

Just here a trouble confronted the Sunday school—the supply of cards would soon be gone! A letter was sent to the Woman's Missionary Friend, asking that packages of cards be sent at once by mail, and that cards be collected and sent in boxes by freight later on. There was a grand response to this call from Maine to Maryland and from the Atlantic to far beyond the Mississippi, and the parcels came pouring in. A missionary received missionary mail in Tientsin and forwarded it to Peking. Ordinarily he hired one donkey for a courier who should make the trip, but when the cards began to come in he filled bags and bags with card parcels and two or three donkeys had to be hired to carry the mail to Peking.

In the spring the boxes began to arrive, and before long there was a room in the mission packed from floor to ceiling with boxes, bags and barrels of cards. There were cards great and small; there were beautiful Christmas and Easter cards, fresh and new; there were rolls of large pictures and there were chromos.

The contents of the parcels and boxes were sorted, and the largest and best cards and pictures were kept for extra rewards and for Christmas presents.

Some of the card parcels were accompanied by touching stories, as, for instance, one that came from Michigan. It was sent by a lady, who wrote that she was old and feeble, dependent upon friends and without money of her own, so that when she gave it must be because someone else first gave to her. She had read the call for cards with rejoicing, as if it were an answer given by God to her prayer that in her feeble, shut-in state he would show her how even she could do something for his cause. She had not known that she had anything that she could give, but here was a parcel of beautiful picture cards that had been the delight of a child long since gone to heaven, and therefore very precious to the now aged mother. Thanking God that at last there was something she could give for his cause, she sent the parcel and accompanied it with her prayers.

Is it any wonder that small things like picture cards are made to accomplish such great things when such love and such faith send them on their way?

There were cards for all comers, and the Sunday school grew as the class before it had grown. It grew until it filled the church, as the class had filled its class room—filled it until all the seats were crowded and the aisles, until the altar steps were taken and the platform inside the altar rail.

Then a second trouble threatened. The walls of the church had cracked and now they were bulging and it looked as if the heavy tiled roof might fall in some day, and then there would be no meeting place. Besides, how awful if it should fall while the house was full of children! This second trouble passed in as wonderful a way as did the first. Stays were put against the cracked walls and extra supports under the heavy roof. Then a letter was sent to the homeland, out of which came all supplies and much good cheer. The letter was received by one whose great heart abounded in ways and means of winning men and the contents of their pocketbooks, and by return mail he forwarded the first instalment of a sum sufficient to build a church large enough to accommodate the work, as all then thought, for the next twenty years. With the money went also a letter full of cheer and inspiring energy.

In course of time the church was completed, and almost immediately it was filled by the still growing Sunday school. By this time the Sunday school had such fame that it was visited by travellers as one of the sights of Peking, and workers of sister denominations seemed to take as much pride in the Sunday school and its beautiful house as if it were all their own; and all who visited the school said: 'There is nothing else in China like it.'

The time had been when members of the Mission could not appear outside the Mission walls anywhere in the neighbourhood without being hailed by some child at a safe distance, 'Foreign devil! foreign devil!' Now the Sunday school has done its work and the cry heard on every hand is: 'Teacher, teacher, how many days to next Sunday?' And from over walls of the neighbours' courts a passer in the street may hear childish voices singing 'Jesus loves me,' 'There is a land fairer than day,' and other hymns learned in the Sunday school, where these children find the one warmest, brightest, most joyous hour of all the week.

CHAPTER 18

Letters To Friends

UNIQUE TRANSPORTATION

October, 1891.

I have travelled hundreds of miles and had many and varied experiences roving about among the North China churches. But within the present month I have attained to a new experience. I have made two country trips since the middle of October. The second trip took me south of Peking through a district that has been flooded by the breaking of the river banks. The river now runs in a new bed that it has made for itself. There are shallow stretches of water between the north bank and the deeper current. My carter put me into a boat to cross the current. He drove the cart through the rushing water five or six feet from where the boat landed. That six feet of water afforded the new experience.

A man who wore a combination of trousers and stockings made of cow skin with the hair turned in, all dripping as to this garment, and dirty as to the whole of him, but large as to stature, and good-natured, backed up to the boat and said, "Get on my back," or words to that effect, for he spoke in the Chinese tongue. I had seen the operation which he evidently had in mind performed on several occasions, but had never noticed just how the details were carried out. So I gave way to two Chinese women passengers and let them go first to their cart, while I watched with keen interest the manner of their going. Then came my turn. I placed each hand upon his broad chest, as far from his neck as possible, then crooked my knees into his backward extended palms.

113

The man thus burdened by my weight took three steps, then turned around and backing to the cart deposited me upon the cushions of the same! No one laughed or seemed to see anything unusual in all this. Such passages are common in the highways of China, and are viewed with the most matter of course air by women and girls as well as by men. But this was my first passage of the sort.

If Merely Just

April, 1892.

One of my girls spent most of this evening with me, and I was much interested in her questions and remarks. For one, she asked me what I thought of a case where one found her conscience dictating a certain course, and all one's friends dictating the exact opposite, "How can one know just which is right?" I was trying to justify a rather stern course concerning a certain party when she replied: "Yes, but if God were *only just*, there would not be one person left on the earth now." She added: "One must be some yielding and some considerate for the feelings of another. One can't be all *just* and *only just.*"

Lost at Night

In the darkness of the night we lost our way. Bouncing in our cart over ploughed ground in search of the road, our ears were assailed by the cry of the carter: "Yes, never mind, only eight more *li*, honourable lady." Directly we saw a light and drove in that direction, but it was only a grave in the midst of the field with a fire burning on or near it. Things were being burned for the spirits of the dead by the devoted living. We often saw these little fires as we rode over the country. There is something weird about the dancing flames and the dusky figures of those who tend them, as seen in the dim light of the night. Finally we struck the right road and came into An Chia Chuang.

Heartache For a Friend

Oswego, New York, April 23, 1896.

For the first time I have a heartache for you. A sudden sense of loss grasped me as I turned from watching you pass into the station waiting room. My eyes fill, as I think of you, my precious friend. Until now the joy of all has dominated all my thought of you. Now the sense of loss keeps company with the joy. When I am rested again I shall lose the pain in thankfulness for the rare friend and wonderful love He has given me.

CAREFUL FOR NOTHING

Oswego, May 12, 1896.

I *know* it is possible "*to be careful for nothing*," and "*by prayer and supplication with thanksgiving make your requests known to God*," and "*the peace of God which passeth understanding shall keep your heart and mind through Christ Jesus.*" The keeping by Jesus is fully set forth in the first to the fifteenth chapter of Saint John. That is the how. The way we are to get is by being careful for nothing. It is possible to "bear all things, believe all things, hope all things, endure all things," and in perfect peace, content, and cheerfulness; but we have our wishes returned to us only when we have given up all. Already given up, Christ will do this. We do not have to fight. We only let go drop stop doing, thinking, planning. Hanging to the edge of a high roof, the child hears the father below say, "Let go." With shut eyes and fear the child obeys, and drops into the father's arms. Then the bliss of quiet content! It is not a fight unless we are disobedient and knowingly cling to what we must let go before Christ can possess us wholly.

LOVE STRENGTHENED BY OBEDIENCE TO DUTY

Minneapolis, June 15, 1896.

My sister came to this place with me, and is here to see me off. She is so distressed that my heart aches for her all the time. And yet partings have only strengthened the ties between my loved ones and myself. It is the thought that the Master gave up heaven for earth that takes away the force of a temptation that might come with the suggestion that this going into a far country is unnatural and unreasonable. Love, after all, must follow the Master without regard to the reason of this world that limits all things to the scope of present joy.

Mrs. Gamewell sailed from Vancouver returning to China to rejoin Mr. Gamewell June 22, 1896, on the steamship *Empress* of Japan.

LOVE FOR HER KIN

Vancouver, British Columbia, June 21, 1896.

My last days have been full to the brim. My brother's two older boys joined the church and took a stand that relieves my mind and fills my heart with rejoicing. Then my brother himself gave me comfort by his own attitude. The Master has added many blessings through the days of parting. Once you said something about years weaning brothers and sisters from their first affection for each other. With us it has not been so. The long years of separation have intensified the love, made strong the bonds, made more tender the sympathy between us. Some of us with unlike natures, find ourselves being knit together in understanding love by the power of the Master's work through our hearts. No, as I love God more I love my brothers and sisters more, and what they are or are not has nothing to do with the fact of the love existing in my heart, and the same power of love working in my heart makes the friendships more precious.

SORROW OF PARTING

Steamship *Empress* of Japan, North
Pacific Ocean, July 1, 1896.

Yes, the last days seemed to me all that I could bear and not break. Of course I knew I should bear because it was not my strength that must carry the burden of it all. I love to think how near the Master comes to those on whom sorrow rests for *his sake*. That is the *sweetness of it* all *for his sake*. My faith failed in a degree, and I was not as strong as I should have been at the last. But here comes the reconciling comfort of it all. He never fails. He always helps. He cared more than I could. If I failed to be ready for his use, he, nevertheless, found some instrument for his use and *he* surely comforted and helped. I lost an opportunity. But the gracious help was furnished another in time of need. Oh, the comfort that comes in the sight of the sense of failure when we realize that our lost opportunities are not necessarily lost to others.

SUNLIT HILLS

Hills Fifteen Miles West of Peking,
August 20, 1896.

I saw the sun light up the tops of the hills west of us this morning while yet the hills to the east hid the sun himself from view. That means that I was out of bed and on the veranda by five o'clock this morning. I should love to take you out on our veranda to look about. In front the plain with its fields of standing grain, and here and there a clump of trees marking a burying

116

ground or temple premises. To the right and to the left, spurs of hills that run out to meet the plain and from the half circle into which our houses are packed and right up the mountainside. Behind us the mountains and the sky meet several hundred feet above the level of our house, which stands highest up the mountainside.

GOD IN ALL

So also, it seems to me, it would be self-pity for me to mourn any separation or other circumstance of this life because of what it brought to me or deprived me of. I truly rejoice to believe that the Master controls each event as it comes. I am so glad that *he* is in it all, that nothing seems severe as far as *I* am concerned. Sometimes for the moment, I do not think of all this glad lesson that he has been teaching me for years, and so for the moment, self-pity enters in; but, truly, any grief that endures comes only from the fact that some whom I love do not rest all things in Christ's hands, and so live in his peace; and therefore they suffer because of my movements, and I suffer because I am the immediate cause of their suffering. But I am learning to rest this trouble also with him. It has rested there most of the time, but sometimes thoughts of my loved ones sweep in and catch me not securely anchored. Then there is sadness for a season.

CREDIT CHRIST, NOT ME

Something in your letters makes me want to write something about this. You credit me with much that positively never was in me, for it is Christ fulfilling his promise in spite of the natural self that I know myself to be. If you think what you see to be *me*, my "born" self, you lose the good you might get from the right. If Christ can do such work in me, what great hope there is for any other mortal! Please do not read anything to my credit in these words. Please let them glorify the Master only.

JOY OF CONTACT WITH LIFE

Peking, September 7, 1896.
I have lived a busy life for about twenty-five years without much time for intellectual pursuits outside of the studies incident to my missionary work; but I enjoy contact with the other life as I enjoy the woods and fields and solitudes that are left on the other side of the ocean when I come again to my post.

THE PULPIT AND POLITICS

Peking, October 1, 1896.

The political situation interests me more than I can tell. I love my country intensely, and so many dangers threaten her. They gather closer around with each succeeding year. Hidden hostile powers are at work as well as the outbreaking lawlessness and greed of gain at the expense of all else, that show their heads more and more boldly. God is over all. If the nation trusts him and owns his power, all is well. But will the nation continue to serve him as a nation? I believe so much about churches keeping out of politics is of the prince of darkness. If church people do not assemble to worship God as a preparation for keeping his law and doing his service as a nation as well as individuals, what is the use of a church in the world? The pulpit need not declare for any one *party* in order to send its people out to act on *principle*, to the overthrow of powers that antagonize the welfare of the nation, the municipality, and the home.

DEPRESSION

A depressed spirit of foreboding envelops my being and presses upon my consciousness. It seems likely that the expected mail will bring bad news. Intense sadness seems to seize all my unoccupied moments. If life were totally ineffective and effort vain, I might feel as something seems trying to make me feel today instead of the steady calm with which my soul recognizes God, and his steady power in whom every effort is full of hopeful meaning. The spirit may not fail today, but it will not soar.

Written on the following day:

EXULTATION

A buoyant spirit catches me on light feet and swings with easy step through the day. Everything comes easy. My spirits rise and rise like a bottle of yeast, and my head may pop off with exhilaration!

Later. The clouds that have been gathering all day are pouring grateful draughts upon the thirsty earth. The trees toss their arms and wave their leaves in glad enjoyment, and every shrub and plant is bursting with intense delight. Ah, yesterday we were tried and scraped with a sandpaper wind in lifeless air; today grateful moisture and dewy freshness soothes the nerves, and lubricates all the squeaking screws of one's system. So Nature's moods depress or lift. Yesterday was bright, today it rains! Yesterday the wheels drave heavily; today we fly on light wing!

In A Chinese Inn South of Peking,
November 6, 1896.

I am to resume my old work of conducting a training school for women. My plan is to visit the village churches and invite such women as seem fitted for the school to come to Peking for six months' instruction. I am out on such a trip now. When this trip is made I shall open school and settle to regular work.

FLOOD

It seems now as if I am to be delayed and possibly defeated in the carrying out of this trip. A river, that lies between Peking and my objective point, has broken its banks and inundated the country to such an extent that carts cannot travel the road. I have spent this day, from 8:30 a. m. to 4 :30 p. m., making this point, twenty miles distant. Here we learn that our cart cannot progress beyond three or four more miles. Our only resort is to hire a donkey for me to ride and let the cart mule carry my bedding and food on its back. Just here the carter came in to find out what I propose for tomorrow. I am very loath to return to Peking, yet that is what I am intending to do.

I have sat in the lumbering cart through this day, and have been covered thick with a fine, gray dust. Now, half way to my journey's end, to turn back is much against my nature; but if I do not, all I can do is to leave the cart here and ride a donkey for twenty miles, in the course of which journey there are three rivers to cross, and thick mud between the river banks and the water, and many other serious obstacles to such a course. I would take the donkey and go through only I would not be in condition to do the work that I have in mind as the object of this trip after such fatigue. Then there is likely to set in one of our North China cold dust storms from the northwest at any time. I am travelling alone. If a gentleman were with me, we would not think of anything but going on.

DRESS

You would be amused to see how I am dressed. I have one of the American storm suits to begin with. The skirt eight inches

119

from the ground, a shirt-waist, and an Eton jacket, and blue leggings to match the suit. Then inside my shoes I have chamois slippers; under my jacket and waist I have a chamois-lined silk waist, and the warmest of flannels. I have bloomers under my short skirt. Then to finish off with, I have on a Chinese wadded garment that covers me to the edge of my short skirt, and on my head a Chinese storm hood. I brought with me a hot water bottle and several blankets, a cotton mattress and wadded cover, and, besides, a fur-lined coat!

Alone in the Inn

I am sitting now in a room about ten by ten and without fire. Half of the floor space is occupied by a brick platform that is about as high as an ordinary chair. On this platform my bed is made up. The upper half of the front of my room is lattice covered with paper. The lower half is built of brick. The floor is level with the court outside and is paved with brick. The papered door opens immediately into the court, and in the court are the carts and animals of the travellers. The court is no better than an ordinary stable court. Generally, the walls between these rooms, each of which opens right into the court, are solid, but this time I find a square of paper-covered lattice between me and the occupants of the next room. I took a brick from the floor to set against a hole in the paper and filled a smaller hole with a wad of paper. These are peculiar surroundings for a lone woman, twenty miles from the habitation of our kind. Yet I feel safer here than I would in an equally rough place in America. The Chinese will do nothing to disturb me.

A Visitor

Just here there was a pull at my door and an animated face looked in, then the whole person came forward. A young woman from the next room came in to see what I was doing! She leaned on the table before me and talked freely and cheerfully. It seems that as a child she used to go to the preaching in a missionary chapel in her native town. She has married and had moved to her husband's home. Now she is going to her native town for a visit after an absence of four years. She said to me: "You just come to our town and I will bring a whole court full of people to see you." As she talked a man's voice on the other side of the latticed partition joined in, and we had a pleasant chat. Now she has gone.

In the midst of my writing of the above the carter came in to say that by going a long way around he could get me to my desired station, only we will have to finish our journey Sabbath morning, whereas I expected to get in on Saturday evening. However, I am glad I shall not have to return to Peking without having accomplished my errand. Isn't this a good beginning for a diary letter? I shall have to close it for the present and give some time to replying to a number of letters that came with yours.

AMERICAN FLAG

Did I tell you that when Mr. Gamewell and I came up the river from Tientsin, in a houseboat on my return from the States, that we flew your little flag at the stern of our boat? My love and longing for my country increases with the years. I long to have God's purposes fulfilled in her. I hope he may never have to destroy the nation to save the people. "My native country, . . Thy name I love."

OVER A FLOODED COUNTRY

Since writing you last evening I have slept on the brick bed with a hot water bottle to warm me and my bedding. I rose at five, and was on the road by half -past six. Tumbling and jerking our clumsy way along, we came through a district that has been flooded and now lies tracked and furrowed, a waste of sand and mud, two or three feet deep. We passed a village that was in ruins, all fallen in before the flood that had subsided, but which left a stream pouring through where was once a village street. All signs of streets are gone, and the ruins are covered a foot or two deep with mud left by the subsiding waters.

When the river broke its banks a rapid stream made a bed for itself through a district that lies in the way from Peking to the place I am trying to reach. We came to the stream at noon today. A boat put off from the opposite bank where the current ran swifter. My carter drove up into the water to meet the boat. As we stood watching the boat from a strip of land that emerged from the land it was an odd scene that was transacted before our eyes. Away out on the near side of the rapid current, to be sure, but in the midst of the water, the boat discharged its passengers! Some came tramping and splashing in with trousers rolled to the highest possibility. Others came on the backs of bare-legged waders.

A wader took the lead of our mule and piloted our carts and all clear across the stream. The water rose very high around us and almost flooded the cart, but I was so glad to be relieved from the necessity of taking passage on that boat that I did not think of the water with any dread.

Just here the carter came in to arrange for tomorrow and to get money to pay inn charges. Here I am, far removed from friends and among Chinese travellers and other inn people, yet I am secure. This carter is a stranger to me, though known to some members of our Mission. He brings in my baggage, calls for water for me, pays my bill, calls me in the morning, and is entirely responsible and to be depended upon to get me to my journey's end. He was so anxious about the seeming frustration of my plan and probability of having to return to Peking without having reached my objective point that he spent yesterday evening in running through the streets to different inns looking for carters from this direction that he might learn surely of the condition of the roads.

He spent so much time going about that he did not get any supper, and had nothing to eat until today at eleven o'clock. He found a carter who had come from here and who told him about the roads, and so we came on. I wanted to be at our chapel at Han Tsun to spend this night and be ready for the Sabbath service there. I never before was obliged to arrive on the Sabbath day. I am sorry enough. I shall be off by five in the morning, and hope to arrive at nine, and be in time to avoid disturbing any meeting by my arrival. . . .

I am in an inn that is about fifteen miles from my Peking home.

CAUSE OF THE FLOOD

Since I have written so much of this trip for you, I must give you the sequel. I reached my destination about half-past nine Sunday morning. I got settled before meeting time; attended meeting; spent most of the afternoon talking to the women and the native helper, then spent the evening with the helper, making plans for women to come to Peking. This helper tells me that the floods came *because the people cut the banks of the river!* The railroad from Tientsin to Peking is to pass this way. The embankment was nearly completed. The telegraph poles make a straight line through the country, following the lines to be taken by the trains. The cutting of the banks is currently reported to be at the instigation of a high-grade official, whose special duty is to keep the river within its banks. He hates the railroads. As the cutting was at a point that let the floods sweep against the embankment, destroying it for a long distance, it is easy to believe the story exactly correct.

AN UNTRAINED CONSCIENCE

Perhaps I have told you of a teacher who told in class meeting that when he was ill his heathen mother brought him a bowl containing medicine over which a charm had been said. He must honour his mother, so he could not tell her he would not take it; he only asked her to place it beside him, and after his mother left the room he poured it into a hole under the brick platform on which his bed was made. When his mother came he told her he had taken it, and now he wanted to thank God and acknowledge his mercy, because his mother did not find out that he had not taken the dose, but poured it under the bed.

CHRISTIANS FOR GAIN

When I see how the hope of gain brings false hearts into the church, how the amounts (though insignificant in our sight) used to forward our work seem so great to these poor people, and inspires hopes and desires to make some of the dollars their own, how the money we use seems to stand between us and the people we would reach, by force of the bad motives it creates, I am almost discouraged. But the women who come to me with such motives return to their homes with a better idea than they had when they first came. They have learned what it means to sacrifice for the gospel's sake. I think they think of giving rather than of gaining.

Even in providing ordinary comfort we give the impression of wealth that inspires greed of gain that destroys the little light that may have flickered in such hearts. Then with such cramped, narrow, comfortless modes of life known in the homes of this people there is danger of creating feelings of needs which they have no means of satisfying.

Then, if these things be successfully guarded against, we are still in danger of giving the impression of great wealth by what seems to us most modest expenditure, and so lead the people to be looking for chances to get a part of the wealth for personal use. This may give some idea of the perplexities that gather about our work at every stage, and yet are not often mentioned.

BABES IN CHRIST

Well, it is just so about the reception of the gospel in all directions among the heathen. We come telling the glad story, heralding a great deliverance, announcing a great light. We know the full meaning of the story, we know how great the deliverance, we know how glorious the light, but we forget how often we have heard the story; we forget that we always knew of the great deliverance and that the knowledge has made us largely what we are; we forget that the light has flooded all our way. And so we expect the heathen to rejoice and abound in works of gratitude as we should if, knowing all and desiring all, yet deprived of all, it were suddenly brought into our lives.

Missionaries learn that it is not enough that the heathen *hear*. Hearing all, they understand only in part. The understanding requires growth. And want of full understanding allows wrong motives and false views to guide many days and acts. The converted heathen is an infant indeed; and some seem never to outgrow their infancy.

IDEALISED

Peking, February 26, 1897.

I do smile in mixed sadness and amusement to see how you idealize me and my doings. I used to have a feeling of insecurity, as if on a pedestal from which I must sooner or later have a fall, but I am growing accustomed to the precarious position and to a sense of security from the assurance that the same love that put me there is supporting me in stable equilibrium, and so far from falling, I cannot get down if I would!

SANTA CLAUS

I have recently read criticisms concerning Santa Claus that contain suggestions worth attention, I think. It is possible to carry the merry-making idea too far now, and the Christ Child does seem neglected in the putting of Santa Claus so prominently to the front on the very anniversary of His birth. The Santa Claus idea would be a difficult one to explain to a people who have a kitchen god to propitiate once a year, and many other deified men in their pantheon. The plan of giving to the poor on Christmas seems to give the Sunday school more pleasure than elaborate preparations for the pupils alone. It certainly puts Christmas emphasis in the right place. . . . I found a class of twelve women. I dismissed all but five by the end of January, and gave all my time to the latter.

Dust Storm

Under the Bank of the Pei Ho in a Dust Storm,
Noon, April 21, 1897,

In all my travel in China for the past twenty-five years I now for the first time encounter a North China dust storm on the river. That so common an experience should have been so long escaped is due to the fact that I have generally chosen a more certain, if more tiresome, Peking cart for my journey rather than a slow river boat. The carts move on in spite of the worst dust storm. I have been in carts when the dust was so thick at times that the lead mule of the tandem team was invisible because of the cloud of dust in which we moved! Boats become unmanageable in high winds. High out of the water and flat bottomed, they are likely to capsize, so they must tie up. From noon yesterday until noon today the air has been thick with dust.

All yesterday afternoon the sun was obscured by the dust until the light was dim like twilight. The wind howled, and the water was high against the boat, boiling from bank to bank. Swash, rush, roar, rattle and bang—the incessant noises have kept up for twenty-four hours. I have on my bed a honeycomb bedspread. The dust settled there as everywhere else so thick that the irregularities of the pattern were filled in and obliterated under the fine covering of gray dust, fine like fine flour. I held the paper I read on a slant to prevent a covering of dust from obscuring the print. Some were highly coloured *Home Journals*. The covers were so thickly covered with dust that all colouring was invisible.

The floor under my feet, the trunks, chairs, and everything in

125

the boat were padded at least a quarter of an inch thick with the sifting, gray, all-pervading dust. I tied my head up in a double thickness of white cotton—a flour bag by the way. Presently I stopped to pick up something, and there was a landslide from the top of my head—a very great quantity of moving sand in the shape of dust had lodged. I covered myself with a close-woven waterproof, that answers very well the purpose of a duster. I drew on my gloves and have worn them constantly. It is inconvenient to write with gloves on, but the gloves save the irritation that contact of the hands with dust produces. When I retired last night I removed my waterproof and shook off the covering of dust from the bed, and with head still tied up crawled in. Pillows, bed, and all else were soon covered again with the gray dust, thick and fine.

I could not uncover food and have it fit to eat, so I satisfied myself until evening with a piece of sweet chocolate and some raisins. Then I had a cup of coffee and some bread and butter. By keeping the cup upside down until the moment I could pour and drink, and by spreading the butter on the bread under cover of a sheet of paper, I managed to get a lunch without *very much* dust.

The Great Wall

October 9, 1899.

I am two days distant by cart from Peking, and a very rough road lies between. It is through the north pass and penetrates the Great Wall which lies in view from the road, rising over mountain peaks and descending into valleys in a most marvellous manner. Battlemented towers add to the picturesqueness of its outline. Tomorrow I start home, and travel another two days through picturesque scenes that would be more enjoyable if there were not so much dust and wind.

In a Camel Inn

I was somewhat belated at noon on the way up, and, accordingly, did not reach the usual nooning place. Instead, my cart drew into a camel inn. While I was there hundreds of camels came and went, feeding at long stone troughs laid end to end under the edge of the terrace. On the terrace half a dozen men were kept busy, cutting fodder for the animals. The feed storehouses lay close under the shoulder of the mountain that rose at that point. It was too poor a place to be called by so poor a name as a hut. Half the floor place was occupied by an earth platform beaten hard to the height of about two and a half feet. It was from side to side of the room and backed against the back wall.

They had made ready for me by spreading a clean straw mat over this substitute for bed, chairs, and table. The mat was not large enough to conceal a heap of most vile-looking cotton. It was gray and black and lumpy with much use, and looked as if it might crawl. But it didn't. So I ate my lunch and tried not to see more than I had to. A sudden noise made me turn as I stood and ate. There was a huge camel just at the door. He had thrust open the door in an attempt to munch a broom on which still hung some grains of broom corn. If he had come in, there would have been no room for me. Fortunately he was tied by a strong rope made fast to a skewer thrust through his nose; besides, his humps rose much higher than the door. Even he must have seen that to enter was impossible, as it was undesirable.

A Gift of Eggs

Today I visited a village near here to call upon a possible candidate for the training school. On leaving, the old lady insisted on presenting me with about one hundred eggs! With sublime inconsequence she insisted upon my acceptance in spite of the bouncing and bumping that she knew lay between me and my Peking home. I protested as I had no fancy for a baptism of eggs for myself or my belongings. Finally she put about two dozen into a little bag and ran after me to the cart with them. The carter did not fancy the gift more than I did. He no doubt had visions of a cart damaged by broken eggs. The Chinese preacher was with us. He was about to mount his donkey. The carter said: "Give the eggs to the preacher. They will make a soft seat for him." Finally the carter put an end to the contest by placing the bag of eggs into the bosom of his voluminous garment, and his tightly drawn girdle kept them in place.

Misery in a Tea-House

Later. Now I do wish you could see me. No words can do the situation justice, yet I shall try to give you a peep into it. Maybe I thought the hut a few days ago the bottom notch of misery! Today I have learned that one had not reached the last possibility of discomfort if one at the end of a dusty, rough, exhausting day of travel, may have a room to one's self, even if the room be a hut and surrounded by munching dust-ladened camels.

Today at noon my cart drew up at a wayside inn, where I had been told I could get some sort of a room and hot water for my coffeepot and feed for the mule. What I found was a smoke-blackened shed, with whole front open, full of men, some smoking. A big pot was set in low masonry against an earthen, brick-paved platform, through which a flue under the pot made its way. I was hot, dusty, and tired almost to the point of exhaustion. Oh for a room and a few minutes of quiet!

They spread some bedding that looked as if it had not been washed in ten years on this hot *k'ang*, or brick bed, and invited me to mount and rest. And the crowd meant to have a good look at me.

I had come thump, bump, jerk and rattle-bang half way down this picturesque but rough pass. The only mitigating circumstance of the situation was a soft-voiced woman who took me by the hand and said in so kind a tone: "You are so very tired; do rest." I sat on a box and rested my head upon my arms thrown over my travelling bag which stood on the edge of that ovenlike *k'ang*, to which all voices invited my unwilling body to rest. So I sat, and old as I am, and experienced as I think I am, I could not prevent a few tears wetting that same bag. But my eyes were shut and so the dirt and horror were shut out. I remembered that it was just the hour for our noonday prayer meeting in Peking, and the memory let in many restful thoughts. I lifted my head, mounted the *k'ang* and proceeded to open my lunch.

A Ministering Spirit

Home. I wrote these last pages seated on the *k'ang* in that wayside tea shed. The lovely woman sat beside me much interested in seeing me write. She wanted to know what it was all about. I told her I was telling my sister about her kindness to me. She asked: "Is your sister in Peking?" She was much impressed when I told her of the long journey the letter must make to reach you.

In the painting of "Christ before Pilate" by Munkacsy, an impressive feature is a sweet-faced woman who holds a baby and stands in a corner, looking timidly and yet so kindly at Christ. Something about this gentle woman in that wayside shed reminded me of that face in the picture, both in striking contrast with their surroundings, both furnishing a sweet note in the midst of a very harsh discord.

CHINA—OLD AND NEW—WALL OF PEKING

CHAPTER 19

Her Story of the Siege

THE GATHERING STORM

This and all subsequent chapters relating to the siege are entirely from the pen of Mrs. Gamewell.

In a scrapbook among notes and letters and other matter connected with the Peking situation of 1900 I have a telegram that reads:

> Tientsin, June 6, 1900.
> Gamewell, Peking: Railroad interrupted. Other approaches unsafe. Wait

We had leave of absence. The school year was ended. The North China Conference convened in Peking had closed its sessions, and our trunks were packed for the journey to America. Certain school and mission matters demanded his attention, so Mr. Gamewell proposed to remain a day or two longer in Peking and to send me with a Conference party to Tientsin to await him there. I did not get off with that party, and so was spared the strain endured by those who at Tientsin and elsewhere for long weeks watched for some word from husbands, wives, parents, children, or friends shut within walls from whence came no message to a waiting world. Mad crowds and burning stations threatened the train on which Conference people rushed through to Tientsin. Then came the telegram.

In the last of May I had stood in Legation Street and witnessed the arrival of a contingent of foreign troops. They were the last arrivals of a force of four hundred and fifty soldiers who were sent from the war vessels at Ta Ku to Peking, in response to a call from the Minister.

After the departure of the Conference party, though the stations were destroyed, there was hope that the destruction would go no further, and Minister Conger told us that he was sending a party from the Legation under escort of the soldiers, to the station, hoping to find there, sooner or later, a train to Tientsin. We expected to join that party. In the scrapbook with the telegram is a note from Minister Conger that proved to be the end of that expectation. In the note he tells of a telegram of the same import as ours, received by himself, and his note closes with what was also the final word of the telegram-"Wait." Who then dreamed that we should wait seventy-six days, or imagined in any degree the. character of the events that were to crowd those intense days?

A later telegram from Tientsin announced that Tsun Hua was in danger. Two missionaries of our number, whose families were in Tsun Hua, armed themselves, said hurried goodbyes, mounted their horses, and sallied forth into the disturbed streets, hoping to reach the station and find a train that would take them to Tientsin, from whence they might make a swift trip to Tsun Hua. But the wrecking of the railroad was begun. The riders found no train, and were soon again with those who with apprehension had seen them set out, to watch with them the gathering storm.

One day a man hurried into our courts and accosted the first person he met. He was haggard and travel-stained, and he clutched nervously at his garments and looked anxiously about as he talked. "Has no one of my family arrived?" was his inquiry at the beginning and at the end of the tale he told. The same tale was told by most of the refugees that were daily increasing in number within our gates and within the gates of every other mission in the city: attack, destruction of property, flight, separation, agony of uncertainty.

A student of the university and his mother hid in the standing corn while the persecutors burned their home and hunted for them. Then in the darkness, not daring to call to each other, they were separated. The student arrived in Peking and not finding his mother there, was bent on returning to look for her, but a later arrival said, "Too late." In his flight he had passed the dead body of the missing mother. Day by day the tales of violence increased in horror. Gentlemen who were in the streets of Peking in the days close upon the great crash, reported that everywhere signs were hung out: "Swords Made Here." And it was also reported that the steel rails from the destroyed railroads were used in the manufacture of the big Boxer swords. If true, it was a queer reversal of the Scripture saying that swords shall be beaten into ploughshares and pruning hooks.

The Boxer movement swept close upon the city, and, finally, Boxers were practicing within the city walls. We heard their sinister horns and thought of the big swords, and wondered. We wondered also about the imperial troops which were swarming through the gates and whose banners streamed from the city wall.

From the Legation we heard of the calls for help that were coming from Pao Ting Fu. Then one day some of the friends from Tung Chou, twelve miles away, arriving in Peking called at our Mission, and we heard how the Annual Meeting of the North China Congregational Mission, held at Tung Chou, had closed in the midst of thickening danger, and how Dr. Ament, departing from Peking in the night, had taken a train of carts to Tung Chou, and made possible the flight thence to Peking, of the missionaries and the native Christians in their charge.

On the destruction of the railroad, the Ministers in the Legations united in another call for troops, and asked the authorities in Tientsin to send a force large enough to make a safe escort for foreign women and children from Peking to Tientsin.

Among the last letters that drifted in before communication with the outside world was finally cut off was a letter which told how in a council called in Tientsin to consider the request from Peking for more troops, Captain McCalla had arisen and said: "My Minister says that he is in danger. I am going to his relief. If anyone wants to go along, come on." We thrilled with the further recital of how British troops had charged down the platform and cleared the way, and a train pulled out of Tientsin with a machine gun on a truck in front of the engine, and sixteen hundred troops in the coaches behind the engine. Thenceforward the coming of the troops was the foremost hope of every heart, and the day of their arrival the objective point of all our activities. Through long days and weary nights of increasing peril watch was kept for the troops that never came.

Following the arrival of foreigners and native Christians from Tung Chou, there was a running to and fro between Missions and Legation, and finally out of this movement a plan was evolved, in accordance with which all American missionaries, except Miss Douw and three in the Legation, with the native Christians in their charge, assembled in the compound of the Methodist Mission, and Minister Conger sent twenty soldiers from his guard of fifty, who, commanded by Captain Hall, undertook to hold the place until the additional troops should arrive.

Hearts beat high with patriotic pride when we beheld the boys in blue march in and take possession of the house put at their disposal. Their presence was the touch of a hand from the homeland, strong to deliver and to comfort us, voluntary exiles in a far country.

Mr. Gamewell had, early in the progress of affairs, called masons and built solid brickwork over the outside of all gates in our walls that could be dispensed with, thus providing against their being fired by the Boxers, who were daily assuming a more threatening attitude in the city. He also had barbed wire stretched across the courts to prevent a rush of the enemy in case they should break into our premises. After the coming of the soldiers the work of fortifying went on briskly. Walls were built across the wide compound and deep ditches were dug beyond the barbed wire checks. Everything possible was done to make the church secure and habitable, so that even if the courts were overrun, we might be able to hold out and make a good defence from the church.

The frames and glass were removed from the windows, and the spaces built in with brick and loopholed. Large quantities of bricks were piled on the roof to be hurled upon any attacking party that might venture near. Drains were let into the church; its doors were covered with iron to protect them from torches. Trunks were piled in the entrances ready to barricade the doors. Water was boiled in big cauldrons set on furnaces built in the yard, and the water so purified, was stored in the church in barrel-like jars brought in for the purpose. Hundreds of boiled eggs, stacks of Chinese biscuits, and cases of condensed milk were provided against the time when we might be shut indefinitely into the church.

Barricades were built across the streets in front and rear, and platforms were constructed on the inner surface of our walls for the sentinels. The material for all this work was taken from brick walls and partition walls, and it often had to be carried from one extreme of the Mission premises to the other. Boys and women carried bricks piled on their clasped hands or in their upturned garments. Sometimes they staggered with loads in baskets swung on poles, and the poles on their shoulders. In the procession there were little mites of children with pathetically serious faces, toddling in the long line, each carrying one brick, or two, or three, according to its strength. There was work for all, and even the babies shared the labour.

It is contrary to Chinese ideas of propriety that a student or educated gentleman should dig, but our students, teachers, and preachers took a cheerful share in all the hard labour. There was only one exception that I ever heard of. A student when asked to dig in a ditch held back in genteel surprise. There was no time for persuasion; military discipline was the order of the day, so the demur was met with a prompt "Dig or go out into the streets." The surprise was not lessened by this command. "Why, in the streets they will kill me," the student exclaimed. "Very likely," was the grim reply. Questioning eyes looked into determined eyes for a moment. Then the student went into the ditch, a wiser and better man.

Two missionaries of the London Mission, with refugee Chinese Christians, joined our number, and the British Minister, Sir Claude McDonald, sent over a number of rifles. Thereupon a company of missionaries were armed with the rifles and each appointed to his particular post. Then a sergeant of the guards put these missionary soldiers through a regular drill every day.

The missionaries and Chinese gathered into our courts were many times the number that the buildings were designed to accommodate. There was sufficient bedding, however, for the missionaries, though obliged to abandon most of their possessions, brought with them their trunks and bedding. Beds were spread upon all available floors until all were accommodated; five ladies on the floor in one room, a family in another room, three gentlemen with one bed and the floor their only accommodation in another room, and so on until everybody had a resting place, however limited.

Then the occupants of the overflowing houses divided themselves into housekeeping groups according to the number of kitchens available. Men with guns protected those who went into the streets to procure supplies for the tables. While some attended to all these affairs others were busy looking after the nearly seven hundred Chinese within our gates. They provided for all possible in the schoolrooms and Chinese houses. They put up pavilions in the courts for the great company for whom there was no cover elsewhere. They brought in food supplies and arranged for the feeding of the multitude. Urgent activity filled all the days, and much questioning and uncertainty added to the wear and tear.

In our courts one heard varying opinions on almost every phase of our situation. One group discussed solemnly whether they should not have remained in their own Mission and if they might not thereby have saved their own and Mission property. There were those who confidently expected the speedy arrival of the troops, and who still believed that this storm, like many another, would blow over. Some believed that the safety of the Chinese, whose number was constantly increasing within out gates, lay in their being scattered as remote as possible from foreigners, while others as intensely urged that their only chance to escape destruction was to abide with the foreigners.

In this connection occurred an incident that illustrates a phase of Chinese character. During those days of dire uncertainty I went into a kitchen where our cook was then cooking for a combination of odd ends of families that crowded that particular house, and said to him that now was his chance to escape. I offered him money to take himself and family out of the city, and I warned him that as things then looked he would probably be killed if he stayed among the foreigners. He turned and looked quietly at me while I spoke, his dark eyes glowing in a face already lean and careworn, then said: "The lady herself is not going, is she?"

"No."

"She is not afraid to die?"

"No."

"Neither am I. I shall not go."

His choice probably saved his life, but he did not know it at the time of choosing. He was a church member, though not much esteemed for pure piety, but when tried by the strokes of those terrible days he rung true, and true he was to the end. He followed our fortunes into the Legation, and was our cook there.

A large and ancient tree, which the children, who in times of peace played in its shade or perched among its branches, called the *giant tree*, stood in the midst of our court. The trunk of the great tree was made a bulletin board, and on it were tacked all notes, messages, or bits of news that reached us from the rapidly contracting world without. During the busy days many a pause was made before this bulletin board with hope of finding there some word concerning the coming troops.

CHAPTER 20

Refuge in the Methodist Compound

In my scrapbook is a letter from United States Minister Conger whose contents were spread one day upon the bulletin. It reads as follows:

June 13, 1900.

My Dear Mr. Gamewell: A note just received from Captain McCalla written at 4 p. m. yesterday, reports him with 1,600 men of all nationalities at Lang Fang (thirty miles from Peking), pushing on as fast as they can repair the road.

That was the last that Peking heard of McCalla and the relief corps for many a long day. Letters were sent to meet him, but the bearers were turned back unable to make a way through the disturbed country. The day of the letter was also the day of the burning of our street chapel, a few minutes' walk from the Mission premises. A great crowd gathered, and when they turned from the destroyed chapel, seemed inclined to come our way. To prevent such danger Captain Hall called eight of his men and charged up the street, whereupon the crowd fled. When they returned a soldier remarked: "It was the yell the boys let out that sent the crowd flying."

That night the skies were lurid with fires started wherever there was foreign property that could be destroyed. The shops of Chinese who sold foreign drugs or other imported goods were Included in the great destruction. A startling spectacle burst upon the city when the conflagration caught the great structure over the chief gate of the city—a gate opened only for the ruler of the people. It seemed an awesome symbol of the self-destruction of the Manchu dynasty.

After the burning of the property of the Congregational Mission Dr. Ament ventured into the neighbourhood looking for any of his people who might be in hiding there and needing help. On his return he was followed by a boy, who, as Dr. Ament was about to enter the Methodist Mission gate, came forward and begged, "Oh, sir, take me in with you." He was forlorn and dirty past recognition.

"I am your Sunday school pupil," he pleaded, and he told how the shopkeeper to whom he was apprenticed had turned him into the street lest the Boxers should attack him for harbouring one who frequented the habitations of the hated foreigners. As he talked Dr. Ament gradually discovered in the haggard and grimy countenance the lineaments of a familiar face. The gate opened to him and he sank contented upon a nearby bench—his wandering and peril among the horrors of the streets were ended. It was this same lad, who afterward in the darkness of night, left the Legation lines and, let down over the city wall by means of a rope, made his way to Tientsin and back, and brought word to the besieged from the outside world.

In the vicinity of the many fires which raged, fearful deeds were done, and heroic rescue parties issued from Legation lines and brought in mutilated victims who yet survived the slaughter; but of all this we in the Mission heard little, until the fury of the storm swept us all-soldiers, diplomats, customs people, students, travelers, correspondents, priests and people, missionaries and native Christians—within the Legation lines. We had a hint of such matters now and then in the notes which Minister Conger sent to us almost every day. In one he wrote: "The British killed seven Boxers in the streets today. They are learning that they are not invulnerable." No doubt that the fame of our fortifications and a fear of what was being prepared behind the Mission walls operated to delay an attack, and lessons such as the above must have given check to what might otherwise have been swift destruction.

A characteristic story from the camps of the enemy drifted our way. It was to the effect that it was reported among the Boxers that a strange being had come from foreign lands for our protection, and had lighted upon the dome of the church in our midst; and their leaders announced that many additional days of practice would be necessary to give the Boxers power to overcome this strange being and prepare them for successful attack. We looked up at the soldier on the peak of the church dome, where an outlook was kept during those first days of riot and bloodshed.

It seemed quite possible that the trim figure outlined there against the sky, and appearing in magnified proportion, should look fearsome to the unaccustomed eyes of the natives, and appeal powerfully to their superstitions. Not only on the church, but all around the walls, on the barricades and up and down the courts, the soldiers kept guard day and night—a band of twenty between the helpless inmates of the Mission and the destroying thousands without. A watch was kept against incendiaries.

The Christians covered their heads with white cloth that the soldiers might distinguish them from any who might approach our lines with hostile intentions. The young men of Peking University, because of their command of the English language, were appointed to stand with the sentinels. When a challenge rang out in English the Chinese comrades of the sentinel immediately repeated it in Chinese and so warned every approaching party of his danger. On dark nights and in beating rains, as well as through fair days and moonlit nights, the constant vigil was kept. Our students evidently gloried in comradeship with the brave men in uniform whose presence gave cheer to foreigner and Chinese alike.

There were three students who were appointed to a hazardous undertaking, which appointment, for obvious reasons, was not made public. When an attack should press to overwhelm us these students Were to drop from different parts of the Mission walls, find a way through the attacking force, and run to the Legation to bring promised reinforcements. They knew that three were appointed to insure that one might succeed, and that it was not expected that all would survive the attempt, yet with good courage they girded themselves and watched for the signs that should signal the beginning of the desperate race.

One day I met our captain in the midst of our transformed courts and told him that I should be glad to serve in case of an attack anywhere and in any capacity that he might suggest. I was thinking of parts taken by women in the fights of pioneer days, and that perhaps the captain might be glad of some such service. Besides, I had been in the midst of an affair in West China some years before, wherein I had discovered that one could be badly wounded and yet feel no hurt; and in this case an active part in which I could be killed and not know that I was hurt was more attractive than a passive waiting my turn in a general butchery. The captain heard me through and then replied: "The most helpful thing a woman can do in a fight is to keep out of the way."

As I meditated these rather stunning words the captain seemed to take a second thought. Then with still unsmiling countenance he said: "There is one thing you can do. When the firing begins you can take charge of the hysterical women and try to keep them quiet." Without humorous intent he had uttered a bit of richest humour. I repeated the captain's saying to my comrades over whose hysterical performances I was thus appointed to preside, and watched the serious faces of those brave women break into a smile that went around at the captain's expense. However, every heart was warm for the captain and his handful of brave men who stood between us and peril.

A thorough organization was effected, which gave to women as well as men enough to do to fill all the days, and sometimes the night as well, with incessant activity. There was a set of committees which went into operation when an alarm was given, to set in motion toward the church everybody in all the courts of the Mission, and to receive them there and dispose of the different groups in their appointed places.

At first the alarms were sounded on the church bell, but later on a different plan was adopted—a plan that gave no sign to the hosts outside. In accordance with the new plan, women sentinels took turns day and night at watches of two hours each, on certain verandas, and chairs were provided for these sentinels. When an attack seemed probable, a soldier would warn a watcher on a particular veranda, and she would warn the watchers on other verandas, who in turn would inform the various assemblies in various parts of the premises; then all would take their appointed places in the general movement to the church. The Chinese, like veteran soldiers, responded promptly and intelligently to these organized movements. Without noise or panic they obeyed with precision and speed.

An incident that was somewhat thrilling to one at least, led to the appointment of one person to each house, whose duty it should be to see that no one was left behind when non-combatants betook themselves to the shelter of the church. Hard work such as filled our days should have brought weariness and sleep, but at first it did not affect all so. An excitement that was like calmness for two or three consecutive days and nights made weariness and sleep impossible. Often through the small hours of the night, out in the moonlight that flooded the courts, I watched the stars and stripes as they floated in the soft radiance from the roof of the church, or walked with the sentinel on his beat and heard him talk of home or the fight in the Philippines.

At length weariness overtook me. A friend put me into a quiet corner and I fell into a profound sleep. I awoke suddenly in a deep stillness. Silence had taken the place of urgent activity. Startled, I stepped to a window and spoke to a passing soldier. He told me that an alarm had been given and all but the guard were already shut into the church. Between me and the church lay a heavy barricade with closed gate. If an attack had been made, I should have found myself among fighting men, and possibly very much in their way. But the approaching troops who had caused the alarm passed by. Then the possibilities suggested by this incident were met by the creation of an office which completed a very effective organization.

When it was finally ordered that we spend all our nights in the church, four women armed themselves and every night retired to the floor of a vestibule of the church. One took to her resting place a formidable iron poker nearly as long as she was tall, another an axe, another a revolver, and still another a patent nail puller that carried a murderous beak. These women were determined that should the fight come their way, no enemy should assail the helpless Chinese in the church until they had felt the force of at least one stroke of the poker, one swing of the axe, one shot from the revolver and one fell blow of the nail puller.

There were many times when an attack seemed imminent. One night we left our arms in the vestibule and sat cm the church steps and listened to what was most fearful of all the sounds that came to our ears through all the tumult of those weeks of peril. Close at hand the Mission wall shut us in and a sentinel kept watch. The city wall rose in heavy outline against the sky not many rods away. On the other side of that frowning wall arose a hoarse babble of voices—a multitude crying in unison. Billows of sound, borne by the wind, surged against the wall, to recede and return again and again. For three hours the air boomed with the roar of a multitude whose cry was, "Kill, kill, kill the foreigners."

The disturbance seemed to be just over the city wall and opposite the Mission. Some were deeply anxious lest the Legations should not have heard it, but there was an opinion against trying to reach the Legation with a message at that hour of the night. Mr. Hobart, unobserved, departed and went alone to the American Legation, though the night was far spent and one could not know in what condition he would find the streets. On his return he reported that Minister Conger and Captain Myer had been on the city wall and discovered that the whole southern city had turned out to burn incense and prostrate themselves, and then had stood and united in the cry, "Kill, kill."

The cry did not die away gradually, but ceased suddenly, which seemed to those who listened a sign of sinister import, indicating that there was leadership and organization, and therefore a more formidable peril for us. We thought the morning might bring an attack, but the performance of the night was part of a preparation for a day for the accomplishment of whose horrors yet other days and nights of preparation must be spent.

As those summer days went by we noticed that our soldiers wore their heavy uniforms and inquired concerning the discomfort of such attire. They told us that one day, while at dinner on shipboard, the order was given to report on shore at once for Peking. There was no time to consider the possible heat of a summer in Peking, or to prepare other clothing than that they wore. They had come in haste as they were, in response to the call from Peking for Legation guards.

The women took a collection among the missionaries, and while it was yet possible to make purchases at the shops they procured enough navy-blue drilling and brass buttons to outfit the twenty soldiers with lightweight suits. We had had no experience in making men's clothes, and thought it possible that the soldiers might object to any fit we might make, but we hoped for the best, and after consulting the captain as to the regularity of the proposed proceeding—for all were under military rule those days—we entered upon the undertaking. We ripped a suit of Mr. Gamewell's for a pattern.

Then one of our number cut coats and another cut trousers. To be sure, the soldiers were tall and short, heavy and slight, but the pattern was medium, and there was to be a basting and fitting of each suit. While two cut, many basted. Then in capacity of a fitter I took the garments to the soldiers' headquarters, and pinned and fitted until every suit was adjusted. And there was patriotic fervour in the pinning of every pin that pinned the seams of those garments of blue, fervour born of the fires kindled during the war that raged in girlhood days, when our town on the Mississippi was always a-flutter with flags, and full of arriving and departing troops.

We found that the soldier boys, sweltering in heavy uniform, were not half so anxious about the fit of the lightweight suits as they were eager to be clothed with the same. The delight with which any soldier who happened to be at headquarters when a suit was delivered immediately appropriated that suit, without regard to fit, was stimulating to the unaccustomed workers on suits of blue, and gratifying as well.

But when the first lot of finished suits had been appropriated after this somewhat promiscuous fashion we thereafter sewed upon each completed garment a piece of white cloth, on which was written the name of the soldier for whom the suit was intended. By this device we gave to each soldier a better fit, and saved to ourselves somewhat of credit as fitters.

Four pockets seemed a large addition to the work of making those close-fitting jackets, so we ventured to inquire in as disinterested a manner as possible how many pockets were essential to complete a soldier's jacket. "Four" was the emphatic and unhesitating reply. So four it was. Four pockets and a row of brass buttons and a little standing collar adjusted under the direction of the soldiers, and the jackets were pronounced satisfactory. Concerning one point only were these brave soldier boys particular, and that was that there should be no hint of flare where the trousers meet the feet, for the soldiers of the marine corps were anxious that no extra width of trousers should cause them to be mistaken for sailors. When the suits were on and the cartridge belts and the gaiters adjusted, and we watched the soldiers passing to and fro, four pockets and a full row of brass buttons each, we congratulated ourselves on our successful attempts at tailoring, and said one to another: "The suits we have made might easily be mistaken for the soldiers' regular uniform."

The days passed in a ceaseless round of activities mingled with hoping, questioning, wondering, and listening night and day for the coming of McCalla and the relief column. Outside our lines the imperial troops swarmed the city wall and streets, and the horns of the Boxers could be heard from every quarter of the city, and fires clouded the days and made lurid the nights.

These days of stress were brightened on one occasion by a call from Dr. Morrison, the Peking correspondent of the *London Times*. Notwithstanding the state of the streets, he came from the Legation to our lines, and moving about our courts, his reposeful countenance and stalwart frame seemed to radiate courage and helpfulness. Later on we heard how he declared in the midst of the Legations, "I should be ashamed to call myself a white man if I could not make a place of refuge for these Chinese Christians," and how he, with Professor James, sought for and found the place within the Legation lines into which the Chinese were afterward received. And we heard how he, with a band of men of like daring, ventured into the west of the city where a Catholic mission had been destroyed, and succeeded in conducting from there hundreds of refugee native Christians, some of whom were so desperately wounded that they died the night following their rescue.

CHAPTER 21

Massacre of Baron Von Ketteler

Minister Conger called, bringing with him an atmosphere of hope and good courage. Besides, hardly a day passed without bringing a letter from him. A letter written June 14, reads as follows:

My Dear Mr. Gamewell: There is nothing new in the situation. Of course the ruffians are still attacking and burning undefended places, but I still feel sure they will keep clear of foreign troops.

I have today seen a most intelligent view of your situation sent to Captain Myers by Captain Hall. I think you can safely trust his judgment.

We have no information today from the relief, but we can rest assured that they are pushing on in the best possible way. Some of our messengers, if not some of the troops, should be expected in the morning.

Keep up your courage and feel that even though you are driven into the church, if it ever comes to that, you have still an invulnerable position. I still believe the Lord is on our side, in this as in every good fight.

If you have any important news, send it by bearer.

     Sincerely yours,   E. H. Conger.

A letter of the next day reads:

          June 15, 1900, 12 m.

My Dear Mr. Gamewell: We have nothing new to report this morning. Everything seems remarkably quiet, and we hope all of your people are sharing the tranquillity.

The English killed seven Boxers last night on the back street north of their Legation, so they are learning that they are not impervious to bullets.

As soon as we get any word from the troops coming, will send you word.

> Yours sincerely,   E. H. Conger.

As the days passed out of the chaotic conditions that surrounded us there was evolved, with constantly increasing intensity, a more definite trend of affairs. June 19 brought a startling communication which reads as follows:

> My Dear Mr. Gamewell: The Chinese government has notified us that the Admirals at Ta Ku have notified the Viceroy that they will take possession of all the Ta Ku forts tomorrow. This they consider a declaration of war by all the Powers and hence tender the Ministers their passports, and ask us to leave Peking in twenty-four hours. We have replied that we know nothing of this, but if the Chinese desire to act upon such information and declare war themselves, that, of course, we will go as soon as they will furnish us the necessary transportation and send reliable escorts to take us all (of course including our nationals) to Tientsin.
>
> We have demanded a meeting with the princes and ministers tomorrow morning, and then will know more definitely of the matter, of which I will duly notify you.
>
> I would, if possible, keep it from the Chinese for the present and not talk much about it anyway.
>
> Please read this letter to Captain Hall.
>
> If we had a thousand men here and any knowledge of where other troops were, we might then refuse to go, but under the circumstances there is only one thing to do. It is bound to take us some time to get ready to start, and in the meantime something may happen.
>
> Keep a good lookout through the night and do nothing to invite an attack. There is less danger, however, while we are parleying than before.
>
> > Sincerely yours,   E. H. Conger.

Before this communication from the Chinese government had been received by Minister Conger the forts at Ta Ku had been taken, and the relief column approaching Peking had been attacked by the Chinese imperial troops and driven back, all of which was known to the Chinese government although unknown to us. It was characteristic of Chinese diplomacy, however, that they should state their case as they did in this communication of which Minister Conger tells in his letter of the 19th.

No response was received tor the demand for a meeting with the princes and ministers of the Chinese government. On the morning of the 20th, therefore, we were instructed to hold ourselves in readiness to depart at a moment's notice, and take with us only what we could carry in our hands. The twenty-four hours given for our preparations and departure would expire at four o'clock on the afternoon of the 20th.

We stood about our open trunks where they had been placed in the church ready to be used in barricading. Tired almost beyond the possibility of thinking, we questioned: "Which of these, our possessions, is more essential than the others? What shall I take and what shall I leave?" Mothers prepared food supplies for their children and others made rolls of clothing. I remember with interest the utter indifference with which I looked upon our earthly possessions that day.

More serious than the consideration of what we should carry with us was the consideration of what should become of the Chinese Christians whom we should leave behind. The failure of the Chinese government to respond to the diplomats' call for a council concerning ways and means of making the journey from Peking to Tientsin, in the light of the events of the past two weeks, gave us no hope that there was any thought or intention on the part of the government that we should escape with our lives. Therefore even though we made a start we could not think of taking the Chinese with us. All we could do was to help them scatter.

Over in the Girls' High School of the Mission were more than one hundred girls, and what should be done with them in this desperate hour? Their teachers called them together and told them how each should have money sufficient to support her for two or three months, and then they were to be sent forth to find hiding as best they could among the families of the Mission's Chinese neighbours. Into what testing of character this hour brought those girls! There was no outcry, no panic, but with white faces the girls and their teachers knelt, and in that hour of deadly peril each one consecrated herself to God. "If life be given, then it shall be a life of service; if death, then God's will be done" was the consecration prayer. They stood and sung "Where he leads me I will follow." Then their teacher followed with supplication in behalf of her charges, and who can tell the agony of heart with which her cries sought God in the black darkness of that hour? *Before they call I shall answer, and while they are yet speaking I shall hear.*

While this was in progress at the girls' school, and others were preparing the Chinese for the separation, there was a sudden flurry of intensest excitement at the lower end of our inclosure, and Mr. Gamewell met me with the startling intelligence that Mr. Cordes, the German interpreter, desperately wounded, had just been brought through our barricades by some of our students; that he had told that Baron von Ketteler, whom he was accompanying to the Chinese foreign office, had been shot in the street by an officer of the Chinese imperial army; that he himself had been fired upon and had barely escaped; and having told his tale, exhausted by loss of blood, he sank into unconsciousness.

The soldiers of the Chinese imperial army had swept into action. The first shot was fired, and Baron von Ketteler, Germany's Ambassador, lay dead in the streets of China's capital.

Swift runners carried the tidings to the Legations.

Other events had been sending their converging lines toward the climax of that day. Dr. Morrison and Professor James had done their work, so that in this crisis there was provided a place in the Legation lines for the Chinese Christians. Orders from Minister Conger summoned waiting soldiers and missionaries: "Come at once within the Legation lines and *bring your Chinese with you.*"

CHAPTER 22

March to the British Legation

Missionaries hastened to gather the Chinese from the courts, pavilions, and rooms into which they were crowded. A lady carried the message to the girls' school. She found teachers and pupils still on their knees and the principal leading in prayer. So intensely was she engaged that it was only when the messenger laid her hand upon the suppliant's shoulder and emphasized with a decided little shake the thrice repeated summons, that her presence or message made any impression. Then with what swift transition agony gave place to rejoicing as all who heard the message realized that the threatened calamity was averted—there was to be no separation.

As the missionaries hurried out to take their places in the forming line each caught up something that could easily be carried. Some odd selections were made in that time of intense and rapid action. One lady, for instance (last to leave the house), picked up a halter, a hot water bag and a comfortable. However, during the long siege that followed, each article served a purpose: there was a horse for the halter, many a pain to be soothed by the hot water bag, and where every one of a multitude slept upon the floor or on a brick bed the comfortable was in demand.

In the line, forming for the march to the Legation, were missionaries who had already lost all their possessions, in the destruction which had reduced to ruins their respective missions. And all knew that when they passed beyond the encircling walls of the Methodist Mission they left the homes there and all that they contained, the hospital and schoolhouses, completed after years of waiting and toil, and the beautiful church, to a fury of destruction that would surely sweep that way. But there had been so much strain of anxiety lest there might come an order from the Legation demanding a separation of missionaries and native Christians, and an accompanying uncertainty as to what course could or ought to be pursued under such circumstances, that the order which called for no separation caused a rebound of relief which made them for the time being unmindful alike of the property left to destruction and of the dangers yet to be faced.

First in the line were missionary women and children; they were followed by soldiers of the German Guard, who bore upon a stretcher the wounded interpreter. Then came the Chinese Christians—men, women, and children—in all about seven hundred. The long procession, under guard of the boys in blue, passed through the Mission gate where a sentinel was no longer to stand, on through the barricades in Filial Piety Lane that for two weeks had served their purpose and over which would now soon pour the destroying flood; across the great thoroughfare which had, only an hour or two since, rung with the rifle shots that had struck dead Germany's Ambassador, and from which his interpreter had barely escaped with his life.

To the right, less than a half mile away, the Baron's body lay. To the left, almost within speaking distance, loomed the huge gate tower, flanked on each side by the massive gray wall of the city. Soldiers of the imperial army thronged the wall and looked down upon us as we passed into Legation Street. Did they think that we were obeying orders and leaving the city, or did they see in us victims of a general slaughter, to be accomplished after we were penned in with those already gathered within Legation lines? Whatever they thought, no hostile move was made as they watched our progress.

On ordinary days this great street was filled with a jostling noisy crowd, wherein mingled top-heavy wheelbarrows, pushed and balanced by straining men, and dragged by men, mules, or donkeys, freight carts and passenger carts, each with its shouting driver and cracking whip, slow-moving camel trains, pacing mules with jingling bells and elegant riders, and dodging, darting, more or less imperilled pedestrians; but on this day, except the soldiers and our procession, the streets were deserted and a great hush seemed to have settled upon the city, as if in awe of the enormity of the crime committed, or holding its breath for an expected explosion.

In the brooding stillness we walked the familiar streets. The hot sunshine, the dust that rose under our feet, the gray walls and gateways on either hand, the barricades, and the soldiers at the gates seemed parts of a half-waking dream, from which our dazed senses must soon fully awake.

At the barricade in Legation Street the Chinese were halted, but finally were passed through and their course bent northward, and on into Prince Su's palace, which was opposite the British Legation, with a broad street between.

Major Conger watched the company of Chinese pass, and with tears in his eyes exclaimed: "We are bringing them here to starve!" Already about two thousand Catholic Chinese had been appointed a place in Prince Su's premises; with their number swelled by this incoming of Protestant Chinese, and no food supply, sufficient for the assembled multitude, known to us, and the looked-for relief column yet delaying its coming, no wonder famine seemed imminent!

From the heat and dust of the street we passed to the shade and broad walks of the United States Legation. The Legation lay so near the city wall that it would be a very unsafe shelter, in case Chinese soldiers should open fire from the wall, as the bullet-riddled interiors proved before many days. Inside the Legation gate we halted while somewhere was discussed and settled a plan for disposing of our company of seventy missionaries, men, women and children, so suddenly become guests of the Legation.

While we waited Mrs. Squiers, wife of First Secretary of Legation, afterward Minister to Cuba, whose generous hospitality neither the alarms and anxieties of many days nor the uncertainties of that fateful morning could check, served refreshments to tide over the noon wherein dinner was impossible. Word was passed that we were to proceed to the British Legation. On our way there Dr. Morrison joined us. As he came up he remarked: "I am glad that you have brought your Chinese with you."

His bearing and words brought reinforcement of courage and good cheer; and we appreciated them the more when we learned that it was largely due to his efforts and the stand taken by him that a place had been provided for the Chinese, and the message that had brought them made possible. It was noon when we finally arrived inside the British Legation walls and were appointed to a shelter in the Legation chapel.

We were the last of many arrivals. Early that day all foreigners in the Legation lines, as well as the missionaries, had been preparing for the exodus which they must make if the Chinese government should insist upon the execution of their order, delivered that morning. News of the shooting of Baron von Ketteler had given pause to their activities and precipitated all differing opinions as to the nature of the situation, and what course should be pursued, into an instant resolve to make a stand in Peking. All of the Legations, except one that was remote from the others, were to be held. Therefore the entire section of the city, wherein the Legations were located, was to be garrisoned by our band of four hundred and fifty guards.

The British Legation was less exposed than the other Legations, therefore Sir Claude and Lady MacDonald offered its shelter to all women, children, and unarmed civilians. They gave every available room, and all the halls and long corridors, of their own residence to the incoming flood. Families of members of the Legation staff combined forces in the crowded quarters to make room in their vacated houses for people from oilier Legations and the customs service. Even the great open pavilions, through which ran the main approach to Sir Claude MacDonald's residence, were utilized. In one, the French Hotel deposited all its people and their effects, and other refugees joined them there.

The piled-up goods of the occupants were the pavilion's only outside walls or inside partitions. As with the first pavilion so with the second, and in and around every possible shelter, the same congestion of hurriedly assembled folks and goods was in evidence. With our arrival the congestion spread to the chapel. We dropped our bundles, big and little, upon the seats and in the corners; and an overflow of mattresses and other bedding which the servants had carried choked the aisles and vestibule.

There were now assembled within the Legation lines more than three thousand people, representatives of seventeen nations. Nearly one thousand were foreigners, of which number about four hundred and fifty were soldiers—American, British, German, Japanese, French, Russian, Italian, and Austrian.

The interruption to our toils, given by the call to leave the Methodist Mission and come into the Legation lines, made upon our tired senses an impression of relief from labour, as though we had now only to go within the Legation lines and wait for the arrival of the relief column, for whose coming we listened even as we walked the long way from the Mission to the Legation lines. But we had no sooner arrived at the British Legation chapel and our bundles been deposited there, than our labours began again. Resting places must be found for the crowd in the chapel, and food was needed for the multitude within the lines. We set ourselves to reducing the confused condition of the chapel to a semblance of order. Some seats were carried outside to make more floor room, others were placed face to face and beds spread upon them. Each party selected a section of the floor space and deposited there what bedding had been saved from the wreck.

A party proceeded to bring in from two stores in Legation Street supplies of canned meats and vegetables, a bag of coffee, some white flour, and besides, a most useful array of porcelain-lined ware plates, cups and saucers, pitchers, basins and pails, big and little. And there were knives and forks and spoons also, all of which were much needed utensils. All of these things the inmates of the Legation appropriated by order of the proprietors of the stores, who also had refuge in the Legation. There were other goods in the stores which served other purposes in later days. While one party went to the stores, another, accompanied by a squad of Chinese, returned to the Methodist Mission to secure more of the food and bedding stored in the church there.

Though some of the supplies had been carried into the Legation lines with us, the bulk of the supplies in the church had been abandoned, owing to our hurried departure from the Mission. This return to the Mission was a movement full of risk, but more than three thousand people had to be fed, and there was not in the lines enough food for the first meal, and the relief column was not yet in sight.

A series of incidents connected with the bringing of the food supplies, which the Chinese carried for us when we marched together from the Mission, show how very misleading appearances may be, and suggest the propriety of always suspending judgment until inquiry shall justify a verdict. After the missionaries' last tin of butter had been long gone, and there was no more canned milk for the babies even, it was reported that the odour of frying butter was often noticed among the Chinese Christians and that they openly ate canned milk. Butter and milk are not articles of Chinese diet; if the Chinese had butter and milk, it must be that they had appropriated butter and milk from the supplies of foreigners. The talk was whispered about and the reproach grew.

Then one day it came to the ears of a lady conspicuous for her thoughtfulness for the Chinese, and for self-forgetting kindliness, and she explained that when the exodus from the Methodist Mission began, and she saw that much of the food supply gathered into the church was to be left behind, she ran among the Chinese Christians and said, "Go and get all you can carry and take it with you," which they proceeded to do. Now, a gentleman, about the same time that the Chinese went to help themselves, called a few Chinese to follow him and rushed into the church and loaded them up with supplies to carry for the missionaries. The Chinese, sent by the lady to help themselves, appeared while he was handing out the things. They thought the gentleman was helping them to supplies; the gentleman thought they had flocked to his assistance.

Both parties got off without coming to an understanding; accordingly, a small supply of foodstuffs was deposited with the missionaries' effects at the chapel and a much larger supply went with the Chinese into Prince Su's premises. Soon after bullets began to fly down the street which separated the Chinese and foreigners an order was issued which prohibited us from crossing the bullet-swept street. So, communication being very limited, the Chinese consumed the foreign stores of butter and milk, for which they had no great relish, without ever hearing that the foreigners had any lack.

Still another incident confused matters and delayed an understanding, which would have exonerated the native Christians from a charge of unfeeling greed. After Mrs. Squiers had served refreshments on that memorable twentieth of June, she gave in charge of certain ladies several boxes of canned foodstuffs for the missionaries. The ladies called Chinese and had the boxes carried from the United States Legation to the chapel in the British Legation. Then the gentleman who in the Methodist Mission had loaded up so many Chinese with supplies came looking to see if they had been delivered at the Legation chapel. Finding what Mrs. Squiers had given and having no one to tell him whence they came, he went away satisfied, and the inquiry which would have set matters right was not made.

While, half dazed with weariness, we were still receiving things sent in from the stores in Legation Street, and Chinese ladened with bundles from the Methodist Mission, and at the same time trying to introduce something like order into the crowded chapel, the grand climax of the day arrived.

Promptly at four o'clock, just twenty-four hours after the receipt of the government's order for foreigners to leave Peking, troops of the Chinese imperial army opened fire upon the Legations. When the firing began we thought of the party gone to the Mission, and were greatly relieved to hear that they were within the lines. Then came the report that Mr. James was killed. I heard a gentleman say that he saw Mr. James, after the firing, fall from a certain bridge into the canal. I asked if he was sure that it was a foreigner who fell. The gentleman answered: "Not at all." I thought he was displeased with my question.

Probably he was, rather, absorbed in contemplation of a great tragedy preparing of which this tragic episode seemed but a detail.

Mr. Gamewell came with others to see how we were faring at the chapel. I learned from him the very last that was known of Mr. James before he disappeared. Less than an hour before the Chinese opened fire upon the Legations Mr. Gamewell met Mr. James in the grounds of Prince Su's palace. In a conversation that ensued Mr. James expressed confidence that the Chinese government would protect us, even though the twenty-four hours, given us to leave the city, should find us yet within its walls. He mentioned in confirmation of his opinion that within the hour Prince Su had assured him that we were in no danger of an attack by the Chinese army, and that the might of the Chinese government would be given for our protection.

Shortly after uttering his generous words of trust Mr. James manifested his confidence by appearing alone in the street, as he started upon yet another errand of kind thoughtfulness. Almost immediately firing began, and Mr. James never returned. Mr. James, in whose breast seemed to burn the last spark of faith in the possible integrity of a Chinese official's word, to be found among us, was the first of our number to die.

When the siege had been in progress six days, I heard a circumstantial account of the tragedy by which he met his death from Sergeant Saunders of the British guard, who with a squad of soldiers held a post in the extreme northeast corner of the British Legation. One day, before orders had been given which forbade women going onto the firing line, I went with a party to Sergeant Saunders's post. The sergeant gave us his field glass, and we looked through the loophole and saw gruesome sights—dead bodies fallen in all sorts of positions, lying as they fell, stiff in death.

The sergeant told us that on that fateful twentieth of June he was at his post, which commanded a bridge by which a thoroughfare north of the British Legation crosses the water that flows in a depressed channel down the street that lies between the British Legation and Prince Su's palace. About three hundred Chinese soldiers crossed the bridge, going west. After the main body had passed on, a straggler caught sight of and challenged Mr. James. Mr. James turned about, as if to make for the Legation. The soldier levelled his gun and Mr. James threw up his hands. The soldier lowered his gun and Mr. James began to run. The soldier again raised his gun and shouted. After that Mr. James made no further resistance. The soldier took him in charge and they went off in the direction taken by the main body of Chinese soldiers. There were shots fired soon after they disappeared, and the sergeant thought that Mr. James was killed then.

Mr. James's capture occurred just before the Chinese army openly swung into action by attacking the Legations. Among foreigners there was still a hope that the threatening crash might be averted by the arrival of the relief column; and, though all along our lines they were preparing for the worst, orders had gone out to hold fire until further ordered, lest any shot of ours might precipitate a crisis. The sergeant was not free, therefore, to raise his gun in Mr. James's behalf. Not more than ten minutes after this tragic episode the Chinese army opened fire upon the Legations. The siege was begun, and along our lines went the order to shoot. And another order went forth. It commanded that all foreign women should stay within the British Legation walls.

Over in Prince Su's palace a spacious room was given to the Chinese school, but it was contracted quarters for one hundred and fifteen girls. Straw was spread upon the paved floor and the girls sat upon the straw. Mrs. Jewell was with her charges, hurriedly making last arrangements, when the firing began and orders were received to come into the Legation. Commending the girls to the care of old Chinese women appointed to that charge, Mrs. Jewell turned to go. If ever the girls wanted their teachers, upon whom they daily depended, it was in that hour when the sound of the rifle broke forth. Mrs. Jewell turned at the door for a last look at her girls. She told us afterward that when she turned "every head was bowed in the straw and there was a murmur of prayer all over the room."

With a bewildering sense of unreality I heard Mr. Gamewell tell, further, how Mrs. Jewell and he issued from the palace gate, to be greeted with cries from over the way: "Go back! Go back!" How they listened to the ringing of the bullets which were flying down the street, and after an interval of waiting, stooping low, ran forward and were received within the gates of the British Legation.

Elsewhere other women caring for other Chinese were encountering other perils. But all were soon called into the British Legation, and thereafter no women were allowed to cross the perilous way that lay between Prince Su's palace and the British Legation.

So, with a final swing, the lines tightened around the crowded area wherein we were to pass such weeks of watching, toil, and danger as we had never dreamed of.

With our march from the Mission into the Legation lines the

semi-siege was ended. When troops of the imperial army closed upon us and opened fire the siege in Peking was begun.

CHAPTER 23

In Siege

Peking lies eighty miles inland from Tientsin, which is its port of entry. Tientsin is situated on the Pei Ho River fifty miles from its mouth, where are the Ta Ku forts, off which were gathering the war vessels of the nations. From Tientsin and the war vessels alone could come any human help to the besieged in Peking. The railroad was destroyed, mails discontinued, telegraph lines down, thousands of Chinese soldiers and Boxers swarmed the city walls and pressed so closely upon our lines that no word from the outside world could reach us and no one could escape to tell the waiting world anything concerning our condition.

Rifle fire opened upon us at four o'clock in the afternoon of June 20, and never entirely ceased, day and night, until the allies came on the fourteenth of August and put the enemy to flight. There were consecutive hours of many days and nights when hundreds of rifles were let loose upon us at once, and it often seemed as if the whole surface of our walls were simultaneously covered with bullets. Portions of solid brick walls were pulverized by continuous discharge of rifles against them. Mannlicher and Mauser rifles, provided with smokeless powder, were trained against us in great numbers: for the Chinese were equipped with the best modern appliances and, as it proved, with almost inexhaustible supplies of ammunition. At times the firing was limited to sharpshooters, who climbed into the trees and other high places, to which they could not be easily traced because the smokeless powder gave so little sign in performing its deadly work.

One day one of our American soldiers, who was a fine marksman, strode by where I was at work. They told me that he and two others were detailed to watch for a Chinese sharpshooter who had the range of a certain walk of the British Legation which was frequented by the women and children of the Legation. For many hours they kept the grim watch, and then the crack of a rifle was followed by the falling of a human body, and the laconic report was passed in: "We got him." It was a ghastly episode, to the like of which we were well accustomed before the day of our deliverance arrived.

Many have asked me: "Were you under fire?" There was nothing there that was not under fire. The hottest fire was received on the lines held by our brave soldiers and where work on fortifications was being pressed; but no spot within the lines was immune. A soldier, coming from his post for brief rest, sat upon a bench under a tree. A rifle ball, intercepted by a tree, glanced his way, struck and killed the soldier. The seat taken by the soldier was often occupied by women or children. I was going on an errand down a walk of the Legation when a bullet came my way with a sharp swish. I had an impression that it had passed through my skirts. In an instant I found myself about ten feet from where I had been and did not know how I got there. I turned to see a soldier falling. He had been walking behind me. He stepped into the place which I had just passed, and by so much I escaped and he fell victim to the rifle shot.

One hot night a lady went with me to get a drink at a well in the midst of the Legation. As we made our way through the darkness we walked into a beam of light that shone from a lantern across our path. Instantly a bullet struck the ground at our heels.

Before many days had passed shells from batteries of Krupp guns began to scream overhead. Solid shot ploughed through our roofs and fell into some of our rooms. One shot passed over the beds of two ladies, who, if they had been sitting up, might have had their heads taken off. One plunged through the wall of Lady MacDonald's dining room, passed behind a large portrait of Queen Victoria, and tore its way through the opposite wall and fell into the court beyond. Hundreds of shells and solid shots fell into our courts in one day, and rifle shots cut leaves and branches from the trees and lay upon the ground so thick that the children gathered them in hatfuls. A large branch of a tree was cut through by bullets and fell across a threshold beyond which lodged a company of women.

The enemy started fires close to our lines and threatened to engulf us in a general conflagration. They brought in coal diggers from the hills and set them tunnelling mines under our position. One explosion left only two great holes in the ground where had stood the residence of the French Minister and that of the First Secretary of Legation. We were dependent upon wells within our lines for water, and who could tell how soon the fires and the needs of the multitude would empty the wells, or what security had we against fever from contaminated water. After a few days the odour of decaying flesh filled the air. The drifting horror made night more hideous, and roused from sleep even those who slept the sleep of exhaustion. I have sweltered, with my head under thick covering, in an endeavour to escape the pollutions that weighted the hot night air. Surely, pestilence hovers in an atmosphere like that.

With so many death-dealing agents in their service, the enemy might well hope to accomplish our destruction, without rushing our lines *en masse,* as they might have done at any time when they were ready to sacrifice their first ranks in the fierce fight that must ensue ere our heroic defenders should go down before their overwhelming hordes.

Surrounded by an army of unknown thousands, rifle shots like hail cutting through the trees, shell and solid shot falling in our courts by hundreds, mines exploding within our lines, and no telling how soon one might tear the earth under our feet, starvation staring us in the face, unsanitary conditions in a filthy city filling the air with fever if not pestilence—what was to save us?

If dwellings in Peking stood open to the street as do residences in America, we should have been soon destroyed by the rain of bullets that then would have swept through our courts at low range. But in Peking, as in all cities of China, all premises have walls, just as formerly in America all premises had fences. One's front wall joins the front wall of one's neighbours, on the right and on the left, and forms part of a continuous wall that stretches the entire length of the narrow street, and has a counterpart in a wall over the way. Then all premises are separated from adjoining premises by other walls, as in America fences once marked the dividing line between adjoining yards. These walls are solid and anywhere from ten to fifteen feet high.

The height of our walls obliged the enemy to fire high, until they could make shelter for themselves on the roofs and walls that commanded our courts and build towers; and the fact that they could not see us or observe what we were doing behind our walls, no doubt worked in our favour upon the superstitious imagination of the enemy. In the meantime, behind what shelter our walls afforded, our people adjusted themselves to the demands of the novel and highly perilous situations in which they found themselves involved.

Our four hundred and fifty soldiers were distributed among the Legations of their respective countries, except the Japanese and Italians. The Japanese Legation was quite inside the firing line, and did not require special guarding. The Italian Legation, being apart from the group of Legations, had been early destroyed; therefore, the Japanese and Italian soldiers were stationed in the park surrounding Prince Su's palace, to hold the place and protect the Chinese Christians there. Mr. Chamot, a daring Swiss gentleman, with his equally brave American wife, occupied their hotel, which was within Legation lines near the French Legation, through the entire siege. All other foreigners were in the British Legation, though the Minister, or some member of his staff, was always present in each of the Legations where the soldiers were stationed.

There were in the British Legation people from seventeen different nations—people from many and divergent walks of life, representing many different social, political, and religious customs and creeds. There were Ministers representing eleven of the powers of the earth at the court of Peking, and other members of the different Legations; Roman Catholic priests and sisters, Greek Catholic priests, the Inspector General of the Chinese Imperial Customs with all his Peking staff; the president of the Chinese Imperial University and the foreign professors of that institution, the president and foreign professors of the Chinese Government College, merchants, travellers, Legation and customs' students, bankers, guests of Legations, the guards, and not less than one hundred missionaries.

We had all food supplies in common, and certain parties were appointed to superintend the division of the same. To the American missionaries was appointed a kitchen in a court near the main gate of the Legation, and we were known as the Missionary Mess. There was the Customs' Mess, the Soldiers' Mess, Lady MacDonald's Mess, and various other messes, each of which was known by a somewhat descriptive name.

The Missionary Mess served its first meal on the evening of the twentieth of June. Rifle shots were hissing through the air, and we had orders to keep under cover. Members of the mess sat upon bundles and benches, the floor and the altar steps, while others passed the porcelain-lined plates and cutlery taken from the stores on Legation Street, and whatever odd ends of edibles they could lay hands upon. When the meal was finished the dishes were passed through a window of the chapel, to Chinese servants there, who washed them and passed them back again, and they were piled over the altar beside the candlesticks in close proximity to a beautiful painting which decorated the chancel.

Then preparations for the night were begun. The floor space was divided between families and parties who spread their mattresses or comfortables thereupon, or arranged chapel seats and spread their beds upon them. Each family and party appropriated to itself as little space as possible, yet it was soon discovered that there was not room for all on the chapel floor. Word came from Lady MacDonald to one of our party that there was a certain room at the disposal of herself and four or five other ladies. Accordingly, a small party of women started out to find and occupy the room. In the twilight we threaded our way through that, to us, unfamiliar section of the British Legation which lay between the chapel and the students' quarters, where we were to find lodging.

The courts were crowded with Peking carts, their shafts tilted high in the air, and the houses all gave signs of being full to overflowing; but nowhere did we see such an eruption of people and things as met our eyes as we came in sight of the long, two-story building known as the students' quarters. The doors and windows and all the length of both verandas seemed bursting with goods and people. It was a confluent eruption and seemed to have spread into the court. There were many people about, but the only one of whom I have at this time a distinct memory is a little Japanese lady whom we passed in the court.

It was reported in Japan, after the raising of the siege, that ladies of the Japanese Legation declared that during the attacks on the Legations the European ladies screamed and otherwise behaved very badly, but the Japanese ladies conducted themselves with great calmness and courage. When the report came to my ears there immediately arose in my mind a vision of that demure little lady of Japan, whom I met that first night of the siege we were under fire. She was not screaming, but neither were we. I never heard that any Japanese ladies screamed when under fire. Neither did I know of any European lady who was other than courageous.

The first floor of the building we entered was so crowded that it was with surprise we found vacant rooms on the second floor; but the reason for the unequal distribution of people and effects was made plain long before morning. The first room we entered was a back room whose windows overlooked the north wall of the Legation. There was a bed there, but we were told that a sentinel had his post at that window, and we were directed into the room immediately in front of the one where we stood. That we found empty, though we could see through the open windows, that the veranda was crowded with people who had settled themselves and their effects there rather than inside, because of the additional protection of the front wall.

We spread a bed on the floor, with the veranda full of people in front and the sinister hiss and sput-spat of rifle shot in the rear; we lay down in the darkness as we were. We listened to the rifle fire and felt the darkness and the wakefulness of the silent crowd. We wondered what the night would bring forth. Was death really near? Would the relief column come with the morning? If not, how near and what the end?

The rifle fire thickened, the shots snapped and hissed more constantly and seemingly at closer range. There was an attack on the north, and the Chinese rifles commanded the north windows of our building. If our beds were not actually on the firing line, they were rather thrillingly near to it. It was not difficult then to understand why the occupants of the better protected rooms below preferred to be crowded there rather than have more freedom in these exposed rooms on the second floor.

We heard the guard come in, and I knew that Mr. Gamewell was appointed a post at a north window, in the end of a hall that flanked our room and the one behind it. After a while there were quick footsteps, and armed men hurrying from post to post in most direct line possible strode to and fro through our room and stepped over us as we lay on the floor. So passed that first night for us. With the morning came an invitation from Lady MacDonald to better shelter in her ballroom. Several ladies had preceded us there, but on its spacious floor there was room for all, and in the ballroom we spent the remaining nights of the siege. I had a piece of mattress, which someone kindly gave me, and a laundry bag in which were shoes and other odd ends of personal belongings served as my pillow.

Many gentlemen of our party lodged that first night in the Legation, on the verandas, under the trees, on benches, anywhere where any degree of protection could be found. On the second night, when our group of women retired to the ballroom, all the gentlemen who found no room for themselves on the floor of the chapel were invited into the extensive corridors of Sir Claude's dwelling, and there, in a long row, they lay upon the floor through the darkness of all the hot, noisy nights that followed.

Mr. Gamewell had his pallet at the entrance of the corridor; at the other end a door opened into Sir Claude's office, which was used as a convalescent ward for the wounded. The Spanish Minister and his wife had a room opposite the office, which they entered by way of the much-occupied corridor. At right angles to the outside wall of the corridor and opening into the little court around which Sir Claude's dwelling is built, was the room occupied by Baroness von Ketteler. I have seen her in the gray of early morning, when I crossed the court to find Mr. Gamewell, before he should be off on his round of the fortifications, standing at her window, white and grief-stricken; and one day she caught her black robes about her and stepped toward me. We clasped hands. She is an American, and she looked only a girl. She was glad to take my hand because I also am an American. "I am so alone," she said.

The words struck within me a pathetic note whose soft ringing I hear whenever my thoughts return to the Baroness, and the brave man whose death brought safety to so many and such burden of grief to the stricken wife. For the shots that had killed Baron von Ketteler had given the warning that had brought all foreigners within the Legation lines, and saved them from annihilation. Our hearts yearned the more over her because we realized that we had profited by that which had brought sore grief to her.

The twenty-first of June, or the second day of the siege, brought us, for a few intense moments, face to face with what seemed the end. The British Legation was, in a way, the citadel of defence. We had been told that when the outer lines could no longer be held, the soldiers would retire upon the British Legation, and there all together the last stand should be made. We were busy about the chapel, when we saw soldiers hurrying into the Legation and were told that already they had orders to abandon the outposts. The odds against us were so terribly heavy that we were less surprised by this early retreat than conscious of a certain stiffening of muscles and bracing of the inner man to meet the oncoming crisis.

A Continental officer, who by virtue of the fact that he outranked all other officers of all the guard, had been given chief command, had judged the outer lines untenable, and ordered to fall back upon the British Legation. This judgement was met in the British Legation by a strong counter current of opinion. The result was that the soldiers immediately returned to their former posts and, by common consent, Sir Claude MacDonald was made commander-in-chief. Sir Claude had been a soldier before he became a diplomat, and was therefore well fitted for the post to which he was called.

CHAPTER 24

Organisation

Sir Claude, who had heard, before our arrival in his Legation, of the work done in the Methodist Mission, at once requested the American missionaries to set into operation in the Legation the same sort of organisation which they had accomplished in the Mission. Accordingly, there went into operation a General Committee—or Committee on Public Comfort, whose members did much to mitigate the discomforts that necessarily prevailed.

There was a Committee on Sanitation composed of a group of missionary physicians and others who, assisted by squads of willing Chinese, performed their part so faithfully as to greatly reduce the sources of illness and contagion among us. A Food Supply Committee kept up a constant search among the shops and narrow streets within our lines for supplies with which to sustain the lives of the hundreds within the lines of defence. Mr. Allardyce, of the London Mission, was asked to see that all were served with meat in due season, and the announcement of that fact on the bulletin board read: "Horsemeat—Allardyce."

A few sheep had been driven into the Legation at the last minute. Their flesh was for the sick and the wounded in the hospital, and Mr. Brazier, of the Chinese Imperial Customs Service, was put in charge, and an entry to that effect in the list upon the bulletin board read: "Mutton—Brazier."

As days passed and the relief column did not appear to release us or the enemy to destroy us, and, besides, the water in the wells promised to hold out, the besieged bethought themselves that it might be possible to have some washing done. Lady MacDonald put her laundry at the service of the Legation's numerous guests. Chinese washermen were found, and Mr. Brazier, of the customs, undertook that service also, and entered upon the office of Superintendent of Laundry, which fact was announced in the words, "Laundry—Brazier," to the multitude dependent upon their exertions.

Another committee watched and measured the wells to provide against waste of water or possible contamination. A Fuel Supply Committee brought in coal and kindlings from coal shops within our lines, and a Fire Committee watched against possible incendiarism and gave the alarm that called to extinguish flames set against our lines. A Labour Committee listed and classified all Chinese engaged on fortifications or elsewhere, so that they went and came in squads regularly, relieving each other at meal times and rest hours. When there was a call for help from any quarter this committee could always tell where and when available squads could be had. There was a committee also which kept the names of foreigners who were available as leaders and directors of squads of Chinese sent to labour at various points.

Gentlemen of the Legations, gentlemen from the Chinese imperial customs service, from the bank, and travellers caught in the crisis while visiting Peking, served in various capacities under the organisation accomplished by the missionaries as well as the missionaries themselves.

Among the refugee Chinese Christians there were men of many different callings, and when any service was needed there was always a workman to be found who could render that service. Accordingly, when Sir Claude made out and spread upon the bulletin board a "Directory of the British Legation" there appeared upon it entries such as the following: "Milling Fenn," which meant that a Chinese mill had been found and set in operation, and Mr. Fenn, a Presbyterian missionary, was responsible for reducing to flour the many hundreds of bushels of wheat found by the Food Supply Committee. "Baking-Tewksbury" meant that the chairman of the Committee on Public Comfort, a Congregational missionary, proposed, with the aid of his Chinese, to change the flour into bread. "Cobbling—Hobart" announced to the readers of the bulletin that Mr. Hobart, of the Methodist Mission, would see that Chinese cobblers would cobble all shoes that needed cobbling.

With the going and coming of large numbers of Chinese, who lived in Prince Su's palace over the way and worked in the British Legation, it was necessary to watch the gates closely to prevent any emissary of the enemy from entering in company with the squads of workers. No one was allowed through the gates unless he were vouched for by some leader on the spot, or could show a pass. W. A. P. Martin, D.D., LL.D., president of the Chinese Imperial University, Arthur H. Smith, D.D., Congregational missionary and brilliant author, several French Catholic priests, and certain gentlemen of the Russian Legation were appointed to the gates and to the opening of a covered way which was constructed between the British Legation and Prince Su's place. The list on the bulletin board announced the appointments to these posts thus: "Gate: Day Watchmen, North Gate, Martin, Smith. South Gate, French Fathers. Tunnel: Russian volunteers."

The foregoing and many other entries in the directory read oddly when taken out of their original setting of stress and strain, where ever-present death stripped life of its conventionalities, and set human intercourse upon a foundation of utter directness and simplicity.

Sir Claude created a Fortification Staff and appointed Mr. Gamewell Chief of Staff, requesting him to choose such men as he wished to have appointed as aids. The Fortification Staff appears in the directory among the military appointments thus: "Fortification Staff: Chief of Staff, Gamewell. Aids: Ewing, Chapin, Killie, Norris, Stone- house, Biggen, and others." Mr. Ewing and Mr. Chapin are missionaries of the Congregational Board, Mr. Killie a missionary of the Presbyterian Board, Mr. Norris a missionary of the English Church, Mr. Stonehouse and Mr. Biggen both of the London Mission. Mr. Stonehouse with wife and children survived the perils of the siege; then Mr. Stonehouse was shot by Chinese near Tientsin, where he was working to relieve the starving natives.

The missionary women also effected an organisation by which work in the crowded chapel was efficiently and expeditiously turned off, and valuable aid given to those engaged on the fortifications.

The servants who accompanied so large a number of missionaries constituted a considerable corps. The Labour Committee consulted with the ladies at the chapel, then left them the minimum number of men servants and enrolled all the others for work on the fortifications. The missionaries belonged respectively to the Presbyterian, Congregational, and Methodist Churches.

Into the little kitchen by the Legation's great gate, we installed three cooks—one for each denomination. A little room in the back of the chapel known in days of peace as the vestment room, was converted into storeroom and pantry. A committee of three young women, one from each denomination, was appointed to take charge of the storeroom and pantry and to see to the equal and regular distribution of the supplies in their charge.

It was not possible for all to be served at one table, so a division was made, and the meals were served by denominations; not that denominational lines had anything to do with the matter beyond the fact that the lines fell where it was convenient to make a division. We had every day a Congregational breakfast, a Presbyterian breakfast and a Methodist breakfast, and dinner and supper were served in the same order. The ladies in the pantry made the bill of fare and set apart the quantity allowed each party. There was an arrangement by which the ladies of each denomination took turns superintending tables and keeping the chapel as tidy as possible. When one table had been served the dishes had to be handed out of the window and washed and returned for the use of the next set; and when all had had breakfast the floor must be mopped.

This mopping was all the more laborious by reason of the crowded condition of the chapel. Tables and benches and bedding and bundles had to be piled so that one section might be cleansed. Then onto that spot things must be piled again while the mopping proceeded to yet another square of our floor, and so on until the whole was properly gone over. On days when the firing was worst, and we had orders to keep under cover, the children also were piled upon the tables while the housecleaning went on. On one such occasion, a child exclaimed in discouraged tone: "Oh, dear, when we are inside we are in the way, and when we are outside we get shot."

The Committee on Public Comfort came to the relief of the workers in the chapel on many occasions. To keep out the bullets the chapel windows were partially filled with so-called sand bags, or bags filled with earth. These bags also kept out much-needed air. One day the versatile chairman of the Committee on Public Comfort appeared with long screens, which he had taken from the British Legation theatre. These he proceeded to suspend across the chapel, so as to swing free above our heads. Then he connected them by means of a rope and left a long end, by pulling on which we could set the whole five screens in motion. This arrangement was our "*punka.*" With a door in each end of the chapel open and the *punka* in motion we obtained a change of air.

After a time the flies became very numerous. They covered the ceiling at times so completely that one could not see the ceiling for flies. A gentleman coming into the chapel one night did something to disturb the flies that were roosting on the ceiling. He says that the buzzing of the flies was so loud and pervading that he could not hear the artillery which was booming outside. He is a good missionary of the Congregational Board, and the flies surely did buzz bewilderingly.

To keep the flies off our food, which was none too palatable at best, paper fringes were pasted onto the edges of the *punka* where they could sweep the tables. At meal time a servant pulled the rope that kept the *punka* in motion. When missionaries of one denomination breakfasted or dined or lunched, their own servants served tables and a servant of another denomination pulled the *punka*. Out of this adjustment of service developed an incident which throws a side light upon the life we lived and illustrates some possibilities of Chinese character. The matter was known only to the servants and myself at the time, and for apparent reasons was not published abroad.

A Methodist lady in charge reported to me one morning that the Congregationalists were at breakfast and much beset by flies and oppressed by heat and no one was pulling the *punka*. She had interviewed both Methodist and Presbyterian servants on the subject, and each in turn professed ignorance as to why the *punka* was not in motion and inability to tell whose turn it was to pull the *punka*. Our home servant was sort of head man in the table service, so I approached him and asked: "Why is no one pulling the *punka*?" With countenance as blank as a mask he glanced around and mildly inquired: "Is no one pulling the *punka*?"

Again I questioned, "What is the matter?" and received in reply a baffling counter question: "Who knows?" The tone was gentle and respectful and at the same time admirably adapted to convey the impression that the speaker was innocent both of knowledge and responsibility in the matter. By every token I knew that this son of a secretive and uncommunicative race knew all that I wanted to know, but had no intention of enlightening me. How could I win him to a change of purpose and gain his help in making breakfast less discouraging to the Congregationalists? A threatened "loss of face" is a lever of great power among the Chinese. In this case it helped move the immovable.

"If this dead-lock continues, I shall 'lose face,'" I told that serving man with the imperturbable face and square jaw. Slowly his countenance relaxed and then took on a confidential expression. When once he laid aside his reserve he proceeded with fluency. There had been hard words between the Congregational servants on one side and the united forces of Presbyterian and Methodist servants on the other side, and the conclusion of the whole matter was, so he told me, that "while Presbyterians will pull the *punka* for Methodists, and Methodists will pull the *punka* for Presbyterians, neither Presbyterians nor Methodists will pull the *punka* for Congregationalists."

A twinkle about the eyes indicated that he was not without appreciation of the humour of his words; but when the tale was told a stubborn look settled about his resolute jaw which indicated that though he had answered my questions, he should do nothing more. Then I made a direct appeal for his help. I reminded him of the peril we shared with all, how any moment might be our last, how all being worn to a shocking degree, all must bear and forbear, how he had it in his power to aid tired women by using his influence to avert further trouble.

The appeal worked. There was a sudden and complete change of front. In most considerate and conclusive tone he said: "There now, rest your heart, lady. Don't mind this business. Rest your heart." Tone and manner indicated that he took all responsibility upon his own competent self. And no one is competent to deal with a Chinese quarrel as the Chinese themselves. The *punka* began to move at once, and it was the man who bade me "Rest your heart" who was at the rope. That was the last we ever heard of that trouble involving the denominations and the *punka*.

One day a teacher of a day school of former and less perilous times, took the rope and kept the *punka* swaying while the missionaries ate. One overheard him afterwards relating his experience to a group of Chinese. He said: "When I took the *punka*, I thought now I shall see for myself what they have to eat. When they came to the table they looked so cheerful that I thought surely they are expecting something very good. But coarse bread was passed and the brown rice was served still they looked happy. Then the meat was brought on and it was nothing but horsemeat, and everything just the same as we have and nothing more. Truly they do share alike with us and are glad to do it!"

The ladies in the pantry developed great ingenuity in varying the bill of fare. One day there were three cans of tongue for our mess of seventy. The tongue was cut fine and mixed with brown rice, and we had rice flavoured with tongue. There was on hand a quantity of flavouring extracts but no eggs and no milk. But there were a few raisins; so the raisins and a little extract and sugar were added to the left-over rice which was then served as pudding. A quantity of millet was brought in. Now millet when boiled is more adhesive than rice. We sometimes had millet porridge. Left-over rice and left-over millet porridge were mixed with water and salt; a very small portion of flour, from our one bag of white flour, was added to help hold the mixture together, and baking powder made it rise.

This combination, cooked on griddles prepared with drippings from horsemeat or mulemeat, returned from the kitchen in the shape of griddle-cakes each the size of a tea-plate—very light, very brown, very beautiful, in fact, the most popular article of diet that graced our tables. The plates of cakes *en route* from kitchen to chapel passed in sight of the "Customs Mess." Soon a lady of the Customs Mess called for our recipe for cakes! She said that her husband, seeing our cakes, had asked: "Why can't we have good things to eat as well as the missionaries?"

That same little lady gave us points on cooking horsemeat: "Cut in steaks, cover with hot water, and simmer for three hours; then brown in fat and add spice." There was a big cauldron in one of the courts in which nearly half a carcass was boiled at once. The long-continued boiling necessary to cook so large pieces, seemed to take away the wild taste that the flesh otherwise had, and when finally our mess had orders which gave us a part of such boiled meat, it found more favour than any other form of cooked horseflesh.

One day the Pantry Committee ordered a treat, and we had white flour biscuits. Probably no one cared that she herself was to have white flour biscuits, but each had great satisfaction in the prospect of seeing others served with something that could be taken with relish. Probably I should have forgotten the service of white flour biscuits altogether if it had not been that a mishap which impended over the pan of biscuits set for the Methodists' supper terminated in such a way as to associate in my mind a child and white flour biscuits, so that the sight of biscuits suggests a vision of the child and the name of the child suggests biscuits and that scene in the chapel.

It was almost dark in the chapel when the Methodists were called to supper. Two mothers of families were spreading beds inside the altar railing. A large dishpan full of biscuits was set upon the altar steps. Turning from the table, I saw a small boy hanging across the altar railing face down and feet over the pan, apparently in the act of alighting in the midst of the biscuits. I captured the small boy and removed him from proximity to the biscuits.

A tired voice said from the shadows within the altar: "Let him come here; I want to put him to bed." Then I knew that it was not the little mischief that I took him for that was hanging over the biscuits, but a quiet, manly little fellow who was as mortified at his predicament as we were alarmed for our biscuits. He hid his face under the covers and has held my regretful regard ever since.

CHAPTER 25

Incidents

The unusual mode of life of the besieged gave rise to many incidents whose humour is more apparent now than it was then. When the day's work was done and darkness settled, bedding was unrolled and spread and all lay down for the night, pretty nearly as they had spent the day.

Among those who slept in the chapel was a lady who all her life in China had suffered from fear of the Chinese, though she was very devoted to those with whom she was well acquainted. It was one of the marvels of that time that she was kept in peace and calmly free from fear. One dark night, when the attack was very sharp, a lady left her place on the floor and went to lie beside another who also lay awake listening for the fury raging without. In her passage she dislodged a large box of buttons, which fell from a bench to the floor. Someone aroused by the sharp rattle of buttons, cried out: "Bullets are coming in here!" Then out of the darkness issued our sister's voice in calm assurance: "No, it is only buttons rolling on the floor."

Bullets 'did enter the chapel occasionally. One night a bullet flew in at a window over the heads of a Congregational party, struck the wall over a Methodist bed and dropped, spent, into a corner upon a Presbyterian. A non-sectarian missile, surely!

Bags were an important feature of the fortifications. Bags filled with earth were built into walls around exposed sentinel posts. Bags supplemented the height of walls. Bags filled the arches of the hospital veranda and protected other buildings. Bags protected men while they built walls important to the defence of the Legation. Bags were thrown into any breaches that were made in the defences. Bags were in constant demand throughout all the days of the siege, and there were no days when someone was not making bags. The chapel was headquarters for bagmaking. Members of the Supply Committee had visited tailor shops that were in our lines. The tailors had run away, but their sewing machines were there, and many pieces of goods. Both machines and goods and supplies of thread were brought in for use of the bagmakers. In one shop a gentleman of our number found a suit of clothes which he had ordered but which had not been delivered. As there was a scarcity of clothing, it was fortunate that he should find a suit and peculiarly fortunate that the suit should be one which had been made for himself.

The captured sewing machines and those in the Legation homes greatly aided the bagmakers. Women of the Legations, missionary women, Chinese women and girls, Protestants and Catholics, worked steadily making bags. Every day in the week, including Sunday, the bag industry was pushed. At times there were sudden calls for large numbers of filled bags. Then we left our sewing and went into the ditches and held bags while men shovelled the earth into the bags; then we tied them securely to be carried off by hurrying men. One day we saw Mrs. Conger in the deep, dusty excavation, holding bags open while a priest of the Greek Church shovelled in the earth.

With the work to which one was appointed and the emergency calls to which everyone was subjected, all were kept busy all day every day. It was a mercy that there was no time to meditate the horrors of our situation—that everybody was so busy trying to save everybody that there was no time to despair, though the relief column came not and our situation daily grew more desperate.

Emergency calls often took missionaries to the outside firing line, to direct the labours of the Chinese who worked on the fortifications, as they knew both the Chinese language and the Chinese people, while the soldiers and many other foreigners within the lines knew neither.

Mr. Fenn, of the Presbyterian Mission, had proved his mettle when he ran the mill where he found it until rifle fire made the place untenable, and then, still under fire, moved the outfit into the British Legation, where it continued to grind for the besieged until the allies came.

He was sent to a hazardous post held by our soldiers on the city wall to direct the labours of a group of Chinese who went with him. He had only arrived on the spot when he was knocked over by a flying brick, dislodged by a shell that struck the barricade close at hand. Mr. King, of the Methodist Mission, was sent at night with another group of Chinese to work under cover of the darkness. Something attracted the attention of the enemy, who at once began a rifle fire so steady and close at hand that the men could do nothing but lie low in the trenches.

There is a touch of pathos in the story of how those Chinese, always gallant followers of any leader who can command their confidence, crept close to Mr. King in the darkness, content if they might but touch the person of the leader whose form they could not see. A lady hearing the story remarked: "And, no doubt, Mr. King also felt the touch of a Presence which he could not see!"

Another man told us another story while, at the end of a day of peril and toil, we served him his belated meal of horseflesh and rice. The story has connection with the most remarkable case that developed during the siege. There was a Norwegian who figured as an independent missionary and horse dealer. He was subject to violent fits of anger, and always had a complaint of persecution against first one and then another. His manner was so extraordinary that only two opinions prevailed concerning him. One was that he was a wicked character, not to be trusted In any way, another that he was insane and therefore irresponsible. In either case it seemed unsafe for those against whom he expressed his spite that he should be at large.

One day he was missing, and it was learned that he had entered the lines of the enemy. It was expected that the Chinese would kill him. Soon after his disappearance the Chinese changed the range of their guns and the shots were fired much lower. After an absence of only a day or two, the Norwegian returned. That he was allowed to live and return was so remarkable that the inference that he came in the interests of the enemy was justifiable, as it was also certain that it was dangerous to have a spy among us who could report weak points available for attack, weakness of numbers, or even start fires and create confusion to aid the attacks of the enemy. However, on his return he told us that he had informed the Chinese that they were firing too high to accomplish our destruction, and it seemed improbable that any but an insane man would tell such a thing under such circumstances.

It was seriously discussed as to whether the safety of all did not demand that he be shot. But, finally, he was put into custody with a guard at his door. There he spent much time declaiming against everybody in general and in praying. Both exercises were conducted in loud, railing tones which disturbed the soldiers whose only chance for rest was an hour err two at a time in a room near the room in which the prisoner was confined. The prisoner was in charge of a physician who was an elderly Scotch gentleman. His kindly heart was bent on saving the lives of women and children from the menace of having such a character at large, and at the same time he intended that the much-needed rest of our brave defenders should not be disturbed by the howlings—pious or otherwise—of the prisoner. So the good doctor was in the habit of cuffing his patient into silence.

One day Mr. Stelle, a young missionary whose talents greatly advanced the work of organizing labour, and who is as kind as he is gifted, prepared to accompany the doctor on his visit to his charge, and asked that the doctor would allow him to try the persuasive force of kindness, before the doctor would proceed to harsher measures. This the doctor readily agreed to. Twilight was settling as they approached the door, and in the dimness of the room beyond the prisoner was shouting prayers. Something detained the doctor a few moments. Mr. Stelle entered and proceeded to address the noisy suppliant. His address was only begun when the doctor stepped briskly in and began to cuff Mr. Stelle, exclaiming with each cuff: "I'll teach you to pray aloud. Didn't I tell you to keep quiet? I'll teach you to pray aloud." The real culprit, silenced by astonishment, knelt with clasped hands, in the attitude of a plaster image of little Samuel, and stared with wide eyes at the performance in which he was supposed to have the part of victim.

The humour of the scene—the mistaken doctor cuffing and exhorting the wrong man, the right man kneeling and staring, and his own predicament—so filled the involuntary substitute with laughter that he could not speak to save himself. So dodging as best he could the blows, he received several before the doctor's eyes, becoming accustomed to the darkness, saw his mistake. The humour of the narrative was irresistible, and we joined Mr. Stelle in a laugh such as was not often heard during the serious days of the siege.

CHAPTER 26

Edicts, Cablegrams, and Messages

The odds were so terribly against us that at first no one in the siege would have believed that the besieged could hold out two long months. But all struggled to hold off the enemy until the momentarily expected relief column should arrive; and every new day that found us yet alive renewed the hope and courage of the garrison, though every day increased the number of wounded in the hospital and made sad additions to the graves of our soldiers. Hard labour and hard fighting was the order of all our days, and for weeks no word reached us from the great outside world.

A great deal was heard about "inspiriting the garrison" and every possible opportunity was seized upon by our leaders to relieve in the least the high tension of our days. Major Conger often appeared among us, introducing some diverting incident and furnishing some scrap of information.

One day, the third of July I think it was, he came carrying a framed copy of the Declaration of Independence which had hung in his office in the United States Legation. Though the Legation was held throughout the siege by our American soldiers, it was under hot fire, and bullets riddled many walls there. The Declaration of Independence had been struck by a bullet, and it was diverting to notice that the bullet had torn away that portion whereon the revolutionary fathers had expressed themselves in somewhat disparaging terms concerning King George.

At last a first word from the outside world reached us. It came in such odd shape and by so unexpected a way that it was some time before it was credited for what it really was. A rumour had reached us of a messenger from the Chinese government. Then Major Conger appeared at the chapel door, and we gathered about while he read to us a cablegram which had been sent in by the Chinese government and which purported to come from Washington. It was in a cipher known only in Washington and the Peking Legation. It read:

Conger send tidings—bearer.

It was an astonishing token received amidst shot and shell through the agency of the people who were responsible for the shot and shell! What could it mean? Was it genuine? What motive had the Chinese in sending it in? Would they really forward to the United States a reply, as their note accompanying the cablegram promised?

There was a characteristic correspondence, after which Major Conger sent to Washington, in cipher, the cablegram which caused such commotion in the world and was at first discredited in England and Europe:

Surrounded and fired upon by Chinese troops for a month. If not relieved soon, massacre will follow.

Wu Ting Fang had represented that it was Boxers who surrounded us, and that his government was crippled by Boxers. Here was a message out of the heart of Peking that made no mention of Boxers and asserted that Chinese troops were attacking the Legations. And the fact that the Chinese government so readily received and forwarded cablegrams indicated a freedom on their part that made the Chinese government responsible for the situation in Peking. No wonder that the world was bewildered.

Soon after the dispatch of Major Conger's cablegram, a messenger, long gone, made his way back into our lines. He brought letters from the Japanese, German, and Russian consuls at Tientsin. These letters were full of assurance of help marshalling from all lands and to start for Peking on the twentieth of July. July 20 was two days off, and there were many days between starting from Tientsin and arriving in Peking. But the heartbeat of the great, living, throbbing world was now felt by the beleaguered garrison, and it braced itself for the days of holding on that must elapse before the allies should arrive at the gates of Peking.

The excitement of those days was intensified by a succession of incidents. The Chinese, who continued to fire upon us, sent in a cablegram from France which announced the Ta Ku forts taken, and a decoration awaiting M. Pichon, the French Minister to Peking.

On July 20 a soldier of the Chinese army, who had received a bribe from the versatile and astute Japanese, brought to our lines a bundle containing the daily issue of the Peking *Gazette*, from June 21 to date. The *Gazette* is a government organ in which appear edicts and other government matters for public distribution. In the *Gazette* brought in were spread edicts of the Empress Dowager, providing rewards to her "loyal people, the Boxers," ordering their organization and control, and other matter that witnesses unmistakably to the guilt of the Chinese government. On July 29 a letter from Tientsin dated July 22, was posted upon the bulletin board, and we read:

Twenty-four thousand troops landed. . . . Nineteen thousand here. Russians at Pei Tsang. . . . There are plenty of troops on the way if you can keep yourselves in food.

We read and looked into each other's puzzled and disappointed faces. Troops landed? Where? Nineteen thousand here? What are they doing for us? Have any started for Peking? If not, when will they? What if we cannot keep ourselves in food? Why no word of organized effort for our relief when our message had been so urgent and our messenger had risked his life to carry it and to bring a reply?

The answer to our questions came when the siege was raised and we were received in Tientsin with earnest joy, strong hand-clasps, and eyes brimming with tears. Then they told us that when that letter was written the writer had lost hope because of the delays of the military in Tientsin. He thought the besieged would be dead before help could arrive, and out of a heart burdened with such conviction he wrote as he did.

One cause of the delay in Tientsin was that the desperate fighting of the Chinese troops at Tientsin and the successful beating back of the first relief column had convinced military men that a large army would be necessary for a successful march on Peking, and they waited for still more troops from over the ocean and to perfect arrangements for transportation.

After a few days another messenger returned with a letter from Tientsin. He was Dr. Ament's Sunday school pupil mentioned elsewhere. He had been gone twenty-four days, and they had been days of great hardship and peril for him.

Though our condition remained as critical as ever, its danger in no way abated, yet the garrison, inspirited by the fact that messages could at last make a way through the encompassing host, broke forth into singing.

At the close of the day a group sat on the steps of the pavilion known as the bell-tower, whereon stood the bulletin board with its news from a far country. They began to sing. As the strains of "America" floated out upon the night air, in what solemn radiance dawned visions of the homeland! Facing death every moment of every day, the heart had so certainly turned to the home beyond that the home of this life had faded until it was as unreal as the future life usually is.

Now with a bound the sweet possibilities of home and friends were brought near. We joined the singers, we sang "America," "Star-Spangled Banner," "Battle Hymn of the Republic," "Marching through Georgia," and "Tramp, Tramp, Tramp, the Boys are Marching," hoping intensely that they were marching our way right speedily. Having sung our own national airs, we tried "The *Marseillaise*." Then from over the way in the pavilion where the French had their quarters there arose a clapping. British soldiers had drawn near. We sang with them "God Save the Queen." (It was "Queen" then.)

Again there was a clapping of hands. We sang "Watch on the Rhine" with the Germans and their song was received with clapping. Then the ladies and gentlemen of the Russian Legation stood forth. They had a *prima donna* in their number, and they rendered grandly Russia's grand national hymn. And again a clapping of hands cheered the singers. And these airs which were cheered by French, Germans, English, and Russians were the very airs to which their armies had marched against each other in years past! A mutual peril had united their interests, brought to the front the essential nobility of each, and developed an appreciation each of the other. And these singers rejoiced to find a ground of mutual sympathy, and for the time gave no thought to any possible differences.

About August 1 the Chinese, still firing upon us, sent in another cablegram. It came from London. It announced Major Conger's message received in Washington; but "British Minister not heard from." Also that after hard fighting the Chinese troops had been routed in Tientsin, July 15, and that arrangements for our relief were being made. In the same cable came the inquiry: "Is the Chinese government protecting you and providing provisions?"

A messenger sent from Tientsin made his way into our lines with a letter to Colonel Shiba, commanding the Japanese group of our heroic defenders. The letter stated that delay of relief was caused by lack of transportation facilities. That another letter would be dispatched as soon as "estimated date of arrival in Peking is fixed." Then on August 2 Messenger Yao returned, and his budget of news was the most complete of all. In a double brim to his *coolie* hat he bore five letters one from the United States Consul at Tientsin, to Minister Conger, one from Mr. Drew to Sir Robert Hart; a line from Major-General Chaffee, a letter from Lieutenant-Colonel Mallory, and a fifth letter from Mr. E. K. Lowry, whose wife was with the besieged.

All of these letters, or extracts of such matter as was of interest to all, were spread upon the bulletin board. Hour after hour, men and women in group after group, with wan but glowing faces, stood before the bulletin board and read its messages of hope. "Had lost all hope of ever seeing you again. Prospect now brighter." "Our hopes and prayers are for your safety and speedy rescue." "Advance of troops tomorrow (July 29) probable." "Relief column of ten thousand on point of starting for Peking. More to follow. God grant they may be in time." "Will advance in two days ten thousand strong. English, Americans, and Japanese. Followed in a few days by forty thousand more. *Hold on.* The Ninth and Fourteenth United States Regiments already here (Tientsin). Fighting this a. m. at Pei T'sang."

The peril of the besieged had not abated, but there was great power to "inspirit the garrison" in the fact that they had made connection with friends beyond the lines of the enemy. As it happened, all five of these last letters were from Americans. Groups of Americans pressed about the bulletin board reading and questioning and trying to absorb every phase of meaning contained in these necessarily condensed letters right from the hearts of countrymen deeply engaged in our behalf.

When night fell there was a group that brought a candle by whose light they continued to pore over the precious messages so full of *life!* And in the gray of early dawn upon the following day an English gentleman came upon the scene and found still other Americans reading and rejoicing. As he passed the animated group he remarked: "I retired last night to the tune of 'Yankee Doodle.' I seem to have risen to the same tune."

The Chinese Christians who worked on the fortifications called this gentleman "the man that smokes." Often when departing for work in perilous places they have asked that they might have for their leader "the man who smokes." Cool, dauntless, quietly pulling on his pipe, he led and worked in the face of bullets at close range. Probably the calm composure that could smoke under such circumstances was as inspiring to the martial possibilities of the Chinese as a bugle blast to people of more emotional type.

As messages from the coast, where our friends were rallying for a march on Peking, multiplied, the Chinese made advances to the diplomatists that promised help from the government, and at the same time closed in about the Legations and seemed at last ready to rush our lines *en masse*. They seemed bent on forcing the besieged to assume such relations of dependence upon the Chinese government as should stop the advance of the allies on Peking and hide from the world the fact that the Chinese government was responsible for the crime which attempted the lives of all foreigners in the empire and which culminated in the siege in Peking. The combination of overtures of seeming friendliness and of sinister closing in of the soldiery seemed to mean, "Pose with us as friends or die."

Someone proposed that Yao, the bearer of the five inspiriting letters, go out again and meet the advancing army. His face bore marks of suffering endured on his last trip, as he stood and expostulated after the following fashion: "Through God's mercy I got through once and brought good news. Why tempt him by going again when the army is already marching?" Then he added—meaning that he had done his utmost for us: "I told your story and shed tears before Mr. Lowry, and he promised to arrive in Peking with the army within one week. I told your story and shed tears before Mr. Ragsdale (United States Consul), and he promised an army to start immediately."

News of the advancing army was brought by messengers sent from the army, and stir in the city told of great excitement among our enemies. And on the firing line, on the walls and trenches of the fortifications, in the hospital, among the Christian Chinese, our daily routine of work and care taking was pursued as the garrison awaited the oncoming crisis.

CHAPTER 27

Belief

From copious notes which she had made during that historic event and from other material she had collected with that intent, Mrs. Gamewell had prepared the story of the siege in Peking up to this point. Major E. H. Conger, United States Minister to China, wrote her from the Legation, Peking, July 11, 1903: "You may make such use of my brief notes as you please." It was her purpose to include a chapter on the fortifications by Mr. Gamewell. This has not been written, and for obvious reasons no attempt has been made to secure it now.

This chapter consists only of incomplete notes written during or immediately after the siege. They, however, without any elaboration, give a sufficiently vivid picture of that joyful hour when the allied forces of the civilized nations relieved the beleaguered Legations.

August 6. Last night the men were building a barricade in the west addition. They left off at 1 a. m. At two there rose a shout which was immediately followed by rifle fire from the north and west, much in the fashion of the first few weeks.

Today the *yamen* send word that they regret the outburst, and explain by saying that they heard a noise on our side, and thought that we were coming out to attack, and therefore began firing. They also send word that Ministers may send messages to their governments, asking permission to leave, and the Chinese will forward the messages. This is because repeated invitations have been sent in inviting the Legations to go under escort to Tientsin. The last excuse sent by us was that as the Chinese are keeping their representatives at foreign courts our Ministers are not at liberty to leave without orders from their respective governments.

A shrewd answer, intended to avoid rupture until troops arrive.

The Chinese evidently will exhaust all possibilities to keep the troops from coming to Peking. They do not understand that the troops will come even if we leave. The Chinese report that the native barricades to the east are deserted. If true, it may mean running away for fear of approaching troops, or it may mean preparations for exploding mines. However, if they are anxious to make peace, they will not want to do any more such work.

August 8. It is just seven weeks today since we entered this Legation, and we do not yet hear the coming troops, though the Chinese report that all soldiers are sent from the city excepting five battalions of Jung Lu's, to meet the foreign troops. Rumour says that the messenger learned that the troops are fourteen miles away.

Footsteps in the western ruins alarmed our British marines, and they fired the Nordenfelt gun. Shots were exchanged now and then all day. One of them struck near me.

August 9. A soldier talking with one of the Japanese, asked if we had sent out a messenger with a note in an umbrella handle. The question gives colour to his statement that such a messenger had been captured by Chinese troops and had turned Boxer. Such a messenger tried to get out July 26 over the wall, and afterward by another route, and was finally taken out by two coolies who received ten dollars for the conduct of the messenger beyond the troops, after they had brought back a piece of jewellery which was agreed upon as a token of successful exit. They say that the letter in an umbrella handle was a decoy. Important letters were hidden elsewhere upon the person of the messenger.

Mr. Gamewell received a letter from Captain von Strauch saying that the Chinese were digging beyond our barricade in Mongol Market, and asking him to come and see what could be done about chasing them out. The captain had gone into the Russian Legation and there obtained a view of the Chinese at work under our wall. After Mr. Gamewell went over, Captain von Strauch cleared the Chinese out. Mr. Dupree crept through a hole into the ditch and found a bag of powder and a fuse, which he brought back with him.

August 10. This morning about three o'clock there was hard fighting for half an hour, with much firing quite like that on the first days. We heard shots against our east wall and crash of glass from the skylight in the back corridor. Captain von Strauch told Mr. Gamewell this morning that Mr. Dupree at about 5:30 a. m. crept again into the

Chinese ditch beyond our barricade to hear what was going on. He heard a Boxer leader make a speech and say in effect: "There are only a few foreign devils in that place, and we must take it." Then they began to come out. Four Boxers appeared. Then the sergeant, knowing that Mr. Dupree was in the ditch, thought it time to shoot, and not wait for him to appear. Accordingly, he gave the order, and the soldiers fired. They killed one man and brought his sword. This incident set the barricades on the west ablaze with fire. Those on the north and northeast soon followed; and so we had a fierce half hour, similar to that that preceded July 14, when proposals to stop shooting came in.

Occasional shots came in all day. Mr. Pethick says the increased firing by the Chinese indicates the approach of our troops. Last Sunday, August 5, Mr. Hobart addressed all our Chinese church members on the subject of loot, and called on them to deliver to a committee all valuable articles taken from Chinese premises. A large trunk full of elegant garments has been brought in, and more than fifty *taels* in silver.

On Monday a messenger to the army went by the way of Tung Chou. He found his house destroyed and members of his family slain. Some had been cared for by heathen and saved. He met boat loads of wounded and defeated Chinese troops near Hsiang Ho. He met the advance guard of the relief army at T'sai T'sun on Wednesday. He marched with the middle column to a point six miles south of Ho Hsi Wu, on Thursday p. m. He left the army there and came to Peking by a road west of them. The army has few Chinese servants. They have pack mules, led mostly by Japanese. He saw Russians and mounted Bengal troops.

This despatch from General Gaselee was posted by Sir Claude MacDonald:

Strong force of allies advancing. Twice defeated enemy. Keep up your spirits. August 10, 1900, south of T'sai T'sun.

Another from General Fukushima to Colonel Shiba was dated,

Camp at Chang Chiang, fifteen miles north of T'sai T'sun. August 8, 1900. Japanese and American troops defeated the enemy on the fifth instant near Pel T'sang, and occupied Yang T'sun on the sixth.

On August 11 the following was posted:

The allied forces consisting of Americans, British, and Russians left Yang T'sun this morning (8th) and while marching north I received your letter at 8 a. m. at a village called Nan T'sai T'sun. It is very gratifying to learn from your letter that the foreign community at Peking is holding on, and believe me, it is the earnest desire of the Lieutenant-General and all of us to arrive at Peking as soon as possible, and deliver you from your perilous position. Unless some unforeseen event takes place, the allied forces will be at Ho Hsi Wu on the 9th, at Ma Tou on the 10th, at Chang Chia Wan on the 11th, Tung Chou the 12th, and possibly arrive at Peking on the 13th or 14th, Monday or Tuesday.

August 12, Sunday. There was violent firing early in the night. In the midst was heard a curious whistling that was not, however, distinct enough for us to determine what it was. Then followed unmistakable cheers, and the firing stopped at once. Miss Dr. Gloss and I scurried into our clothing and issued into the court to find news. Later we heard that the Japanese whistled with their fingers in their mouths, and the Italians cried, "Bravo, bravo!" At any rate, the triumphant cheer produced silence. Perhaps the enemy thought that the troops had arrived; perhaps their superstitions supplied fearful possibilities from foreigners.

A French marine was killed, a German wounded, and a Russian slightly wounded but not brought to the hospital. A Frenchman who was injured by the accidental discharge of a gun, died, also a Russian. A French captain was killed about six p. m.

August 13. Violent firing began again about noon, and continued with brief intervals all through the afternoon and night. A note came from Captain Hall to Mr. Squiers in the morning, reporting that the Chinese were leaving the city by the Ch'ien Mên. He had counted five hundred in the first detachment, and a few more than five hundred had left shortly after. In the evening a thousand left the Ch'ien Mên at full gallop, going south. A large number of men were seen coming in on the west, and the Chinese there were much bolder about exposing themselves to our fire. Twenty were killed during the day.

This is the first day mentioned by the Japanese general as the date of possible arrival in Peking!

Persistent firing all night. Almost no sleep until daylight. Some did not sleep then. A bullet came into our east door. Entering the northeast window, it struck at an angle the opposite wall and carried a pattie of pulverized plaster back to the east wall, a few feet from the window at which it entered, and then struck the floor not far from the head of Mrs. Brent's bed.

The rifle fire did more damage to fortifications than any heretofore directed against the English Legation. Rifles carry bullets that penetrate very thick walls. Our Nordenfelt gun and the Austrian machine gun both on the west, the former on its stand and the latter in the second floor of stable court house, all ready in case the Chinese should, at last, make a rush. The din of musketry made it impossible for us who slept in the ballroom to hear what might be going on at the west where the rush would come from if made at all. About twelve midnight Mr. Gamewell came over to say that the attack was the same as of old. The Chinese were not coming from cover, but at their barricades on all sides, were pouring in rifle fire. Bullets knocked tiles and bricks from roof into our court, gullets struck the church gable, making many dents in proximity to the stone cross on top of the gable. No doubt the fire was aimed at the cross.

Marvellous but true: not one person wounded through the night, yet up to 10 p. m. Mr. Gamewell and Chinese worked on barricades, and *many* others were about.

After weeks of hardship, hard work and brave holding on, the marines are entrenched in a place of great strength: walls, ten feet and more thick, trenches one hundred and fifty yards long connecting barricades at east and west extremities; three bastions outlook at the ramps, and the ramps so fortified as to make passage up and down safe. One cannot but wonder at the fortitude of those who held the wall in the days before these safe-guards were completed—days when men passed up and down under fire and crept from point to point behind insufficient barriers. Captain Myers's charge, for taking the Chinese barrier on the city wall, in order to enable our men to hold their place on the wall, was one of the most brilliant events of the siege. The charge was made by the American marines, aided by the British and Russians.

Telegrams from Chefoo, Shanghai, and Hankow saying "All right" in those places.

French sent asking *yamen* to let a messenger go to Pei T'ang (Catholic cathedral). A reply came saying impossible tor send messenger to Pei T'ang, for there are foreign troops there, and they would kill the messenger; that they cannot open market for us, because our people fire upon those who bring articles for sale; that these nightly attacks are caused by Christians firing upon Chinese troops. *They begin* the firing.

A message came from *yamen* saying that they were busy and could not come, according to their suggestion, and consult about stopping the shooting; besides, our men had shot and killed one of their officers, and killed and wounded twenty-six men, and we should see to restraining our men.

August 14. Firing continued from eight in the evening without intermission except the briefest. The machine guns on the west, Colt's Automatic, at the Canal fort, were fired frequently during the night. About 3 a. m. Mr. Gamewell came to say that the troops were really at hand. Gentlemen gathered at the church where the ladies treated them to cocoa and coffee. General rejoicing in our room (ballroom), but I was the only one who got up and dressed. I did not know of company at church. We talked and were full of good cheer in spite of bullets. However, the firing became less fierce after the foreign artillery was unmistakable. They say the Chinese gathered in a mass on the west and seemed to be trying to pluck up courage to make a rush, but after firing two or more hours, scattered to usual positions. The leaders exhorted "*Pu p'a, Kuo-ch'ü,*" "*Kuo pu ch'ü.*" ("Don't be afraid. Go on across." "We can't get across.")

No doubt the presence of the fearful machine guns on the west did much, if not everything, to restrain the Chinese from rushing. Mitchell, an American gunner, was badly wounded sitting behind "Betsy," the international gun, exposed to fire through the porthole made for the gun. A shell exploded in Sir Claude's bedroom. The buildings along the west are badly shattered by the firing. The Chinese are giving the worst they are capable of in these final hours—possibly days. The troops are supposed to be the advanced guard, in which case they will wait for the main army and we cannot tell when we shall see them.

A German marine recently discharged from hospital was killed last night, August 13. The Japanese doctor was wounded. Mitchell's arm was shattered, and may be amputated. Man beside him scratched by fragment of same shot.

August 14, noon. Heavy artillery at Chi H'ua Gate. Men on wall watch shells breaking over gate tower. Troops by thousands moving west. Some think our troops are surrounding the city.

August 14, 2 :30 p. m. I was stitching sandbags on Mrs. Douw's sewing machine when there came a sound of running and of voices, calling. We ran out and soon saw the turbaned heads of India troops. On they came through the south gate, shouting, glad to be the first, and who can tell how glad we were to see them! On they came up through the water gate almost on the run. First the turbaned *Sikh* warriors led by British officers, then the helmeted British, and last our boys with slouch hats and such pitifully haggard faces. We cheered and waved and wiped our eyes.

The Chinese opened a furious fire. It seemed as if they could not know that the troops had arrived. A *Sikh* who went to the gate to fire the Colt gun was wounded in the face, and later on a United States marine also was wounded. Our deliverers had heard firing as far away as Tung Chou, fourteen miles east of Peking, and thus knew for the first time that we were still alive; but still feared that they might be too late. They were hollow-eyed and haggard from rapid marching and repeated hard fighting.

My heart throbbed with the sense of gratitude, admiration, and devotion as we greeted the heroes who came to our deliverance. There was, however, a cold clutch on the thrilling gladness when I was reminded of the soldiers, the missionaries, the native converts, and others who were not.

Mr. and Mrs. Gamewell had engaged passage to the United States several months before the siege, and had planned to leave Peking the day communication with the outside world was destroyed. They returned to the United States soon after the relief of the Legations. The following appears in Mrs. Gamewell's notes:

August 22, 1900. Barricades prevented wagons from coming to the English Legation to get us and our baggage, so we started from the American Legation. Mrs. Squiers, who gave us lunch on the day of our entrance on the Legation premises, was ready with lunch and hot coffee on this day of our departure. About eighteen wagons drove to the Legation gate, and our party in groups of three and five were deposited with our baggage by turns in huge army wagons drawn each by four army mules. Seated on our trunks, we started on our way, speeded by those who remain for further developments.

Through the ruins about the Ch'ien Men, or Front Gate, we were watched by men from the Philippines with home hunger in their eyes. We went on through the east gate where the Russian flag was flying, down through the premises of the North China College at Tung Chow, with no vestiges of outside walls or of houses left. At Tung Chow we took boats for Tientsin. The boats got off about sunset. It rained a large part of the night. The boats stuck in the mud and listed so that water ran in and soaked parts of our beds. The boats were large rice boats and slow to move through the shallow waters.

Saturday, August 25, 1900. Arrived at Tientsin about noon. A big mast gave way, caused by bumping into something, and fell, barely escaping crushing us. The poor corporal in charge was dreadfully distressed, because it crushed the rudder and he had to put in at the British Consulate.

A member of the Methodist New Connection Mission was at Wei Hai Wei when news of the relief of Peking arrived. A small vessel came into the harbour at Wei Hai Wei and flew the signal "Peking relieved, Ministers safe," and repeated the signal until it was taken up on shore; and then hurried off down the coast signalling wherever anxious ones waited news from the army advancing to the besieged capital. Men rushed out calling to one another: "Peking relieved, Ministers safe." One rushed to Mr. Headley's and shouted: "Peking relieved, Ministers safe." Mr. Headley took his hat and shouted: "Peking relieved, Ministers safe." He met a friend and repeated the glad cry: "Peking relieved, Ministers safe." His friend ejaculated, "Good gracious! You don't say so," and immediately ran off echoing: "Peking relieved, Ministers safe."

From Tientsin Mr. and Mrs. Gamewell were taken to Nagasaki, Japan, with many who had passed through the siege, on the Peninsular and Oriental steamship *Ballarat*, which had been impressed by the British government as a troop ship. From Nagasaki they went to Yokohama and Tokio and in due time reached the United States. Mrs. Gamewell's feelings about the changed condition brought about by the siege in Peking and the events of 1900 and the years following, are expressed in the closing words of her booklet, China, Old and New, the last words written by her for publication:

> The present crisis in China is a turning point in the history of the world. English rule controls the millions of India, and English and European forces are supreme in Africa. But China is the one great non-Christian empire of the earth, who flies her own flag and rules her own people. If, with her four hundred millions, she swings into line as a military nation, without becoming Christian, she will bring trouble to the Christian world.
>
> Selfish interests alone counsel prompt and generous action in China's behalf on the part of Christian nations.

God has answered the prayer of the church by his overruling, which lays China wide open for the advance of the church. China calls across the water *to us*.

By manifest providence God points the way *for us*.

Today is a day of supreme opportunity for our nation and our church.

It is a day of supreme responsibility as well. If the church moves 'speedily and with large resources' to meet its responsibilities, the cloud of materialism already shadowing Japan shall be dissipated, and can never drift thence to shadow our own land. And our generation may see flying above the dragon flag, the white pennant with its sign of the all conquering cross of Christ."

CHAPTER 28

Coronation

Mrs. Gamewell was endowed with a remarkably robust physical constitution, which in a normal environment would have warranted a reasonable expectation of an unusually long life. She also had an equally healthy mind; never given to morbidity, never distrusting her convictions, never allowing her aspirations to float away into vague ideals which she could not reduce to practical methods. Her poetic dreams were kept sane by the necessity of constant action. Furthermore, her spiritual life was of the most healthful type. Her letters and diaries never reveal any morbid introspection. If she was ever given to microscopical and chemical examination of her soul life, she never exposed it to others.

Her faith in the presence of God, and his superintending will in all the events of her life, was absolute. It covered all her thinking and gave character to all her deeds. She was not haunted by foreboding fears or unduly distressed by the miscarriage of her plans. She not only believed in the promise of the risen Christ to those who carry the gospel to the end of the world, "*Lo I am with you alway*," but she realized it. This consciousness of the presence of the living Christ was the secret of her calm in stressful hours and the occasion of her fiery enthusiasm when exceptional energy was required.

There can be no doubt that it was this perfect health of her mind and spirit that resisted for many years the deadly sanitary conditions in which she was compelled to live. By the fullness and might of her inward health she cast off poisons and walked as with a charmed life amid infections that otherwise would have early wrecked her nervous energies. It was truly her faith that enabled her "to tread on serpents and scorpions, and to drink the deadly thing and not be hurt by it."

But only one robed in immortality could forever withstand the

193

poisonous shafts that pierced her mortal flesh. The air she breathed was nauseating with the odours of decay, and thick with dust that carried the *pestilence that walketh by day*. When at home her outlook was bounded by the brick walls of the Mission compound. When she stepped out of its gates she moved into that awful spirit of heathendom, which is impossible to define but is so oppressively real. Then her mission brought her in daily contact with unhappiness, pain, and sin which she was helpless to relieve. She witnessed oppression and vice in dreadful forms, and knew that the only hope of recovery was in the Christ whom these people rejected. It would require nerves of steel and a heart of stone to endure this day by day without breaking. To have gone to the stake would have been an easy task. But her life was being consumed by slow fires.

An anaemic condition made her work at times very exhausting and occasionally threatened serious consequences. It was decided that she should return to the United States for special medical treatment and for a period of rest. But before she could complete her arrangements, the siege occurred and she was compelled to witness the obliteration of every material result of all her years of toil in North China, just as several years before, she had seen it wiped out in West China. After this came the horror of those eight long weeks of siege in the British Legation. There is a point when the strain will break the strongest cable, and it is a wonder that her heroic spirit did not succumb at that time. But August 14 brought relief, and eight days later Mrs. Gamewell left the city never to return.

After Mr. and Mrs. Gamewell had come to America, her health seemed to improve, and they planned, as soon as the way opened, to return to their work in China, even going so far as to purchase furniture and books, and packing them for shipping. But in every instance, just before fixing the time, there would occur some threatening symptoms in her condition which compelled the postponement of the date.

In the meanwhile Mr. Gamewell was appointed by the Missionary Board of the Methodist Episcopal Church as Field Secretary and afterward Executive Secretary of the Open Door Commission, having his office in New York city. During the greater part of their time he and Mrs. Gamewell made their home with his sister, Mrs. A. H. Tuttle, Summit, New Jersey.

During these years of enfeebled health, Mrs. Gamewell was indefatigable in labour. While she conscientiously followed the counsel of her medical advisers, and at one time spent nearly an entire year in retirement under treatment in a sanatorium, her unimpaired spiritual force made it impossible for her to be idle. It is astonishing what an enormous amount of work this brave woman did after her return from China.

She was constantly travelling over the country, addressing conventions and Conferences, organizing auxiliaries, and striving by personal interviews to awaken the people to an appreciation of the supreme importance of this hour in the redemption of China.

And her skilful pen was ever busy. She wrote a number of charming tracts on subjects relating to the work of God in China. Two articles in The Chautauquan entitled respectively, *From Sea to Peking* and *Up the Yangtse to Thibet*, are of historical value. A booklet entitled *China, New and Old*, reads like a romance and has had an immense circulation. Her most elaborate work, on which she was toiling when her pen fell from her hand, is an account of the siege in Peking, published in this volume. The story had been written out from her notes and is published without revision.

The following extracts from personal letters to friends give but a suggestion of the spirit of her mind. They might well be called *airelles*, which are flowers of Russia, the fruit of which is said to ripen in October, but grows sweet only by lying under the winter snow:

A certain chord is audible in the soul of the needy. Divine love and wish uniting with human wish and prayer makes the harmony of chord that alone can reach the other soul. So God must have human fitness in order to reach other human need.

I suppose torn and threadbare linen would make, in the hands of the manufacturer, as fine a piece of paper as right new linen. So a torn and damaged life left in His hands, may come forth at last a fair, clear page on which beautiful things may yet be written.

You still cling to some idea of your own fitness, and having missed the fitness you might have had, you think God's perfect work cannot be done in your character. The fact is that if your life had, from the beginning, been perfect, it would count *nothing* as fitness. It is loyalty, love, adoration that throws all at his feet with *never a thought of self, fit or unfit*, full of absorbing thought of him and outgoing to himonly these that count fitness. The bigger the failure of the life cast at his feet has been the more intense the rapture before the presence of the divine Master.

It seems a small thing to trust the outcome of the greatest issues of our day to Him whose love and power are so mighty as compared with any force that this world can produce to try His might. And it seems a great thing to rest our little cares upon One whose love and infinite wisdom guides systems of worlds in their courses as easily as He guides our lives through their little rounds.

The story of the man who was blind from his birth is one of the sweetest in the Bible (John 9. 1-38).

He was loyal to Him who cured his blindness though he did not know who He was, and though learned men denounced 'the man called Jesus,' the ignorant beggar, full of loyalty, said: 'He is a prophet.' Though his parents feared, he stood firm and suffered the worst that a Jew could bear. 'They cast him out.' Then 'Jesus heard, Jesus found him,' and then followed that tender dialogue, and the loyal heart of the beggar bowed in adoration before his Lord. Direct, loyal, true, knowing only that the good done to him could not have been done by a bad man, he stood firmly by that truth, and the result was that Jesus found him, came to him, and the ignorant beggar gloried in a revelation that the learned could not receive. I almost imagine I see the depth of tenderness in Christ's face when he looked on one so lowly who had been 'faithful over a few things,' faithful to his limited revelation, and so made the recipient of a fuller revelation.

On the whole, a tree is the most sympathetic object in nature, not so awfully set as the mountains, not so fickle and treacherous as the sea, more substantial than the clouds, not so perishable as the grass and flowers—always there, steadfast and strong, with its shifting lights and shadows, soft sighing or brisk tossing, or drenched brightness, seeming to enter into every mood of its friends. It sighs sympathy, whispers peace, murmurs comfort, waves refreshment, or shouts exhilaratingly, according to whether the breeze be gentle or high, whether the day be bright or dripping.

Come out among the flowers and sunshine of Christ's spiritual garden, full of the beauty of his presence, quivering with inspiration from heaven. The soul walking there, listening for the voice of the Master, forgets the worm, self, that crawls, perhaps, across his path. It does not occur to him that it is worthwhile to him even to step and crush the little creature, but with a smile of pity he leaves it crawling there and goes his way full of the Master's commission. Self dies while the soul works for other souls.

I believe we *must* leave the killing of self to the Master. If we undertake the work, we shall do mischief, and perhaps bring our own souls into spiritual ill health, if not our minds into unstable equilibrium.

Talents may be *revelations of truth* as well as powers of mind or body. Indeed, I think such an interpretation floods the parable of the talents with meaning and inspiration. Read the story of the blind man (John 9. 1-35) and the parable of the talents (Matt. 25. 14-30) together and see if you do not agree with me. Do you not see that using one truth helps to the understanding of a deeper truth? And so knowledge unto everyone that hath shall be given, but from him that hath not shall be taken away even that which he hath.

When another looks through the bent, unlovely life and says in effect, 'I know your ideals are high and true, I know you try for the best only,' one forgets the pain of her own unloveliness in the sweet sense of comradeship in the presence of a kindred spirit. It is by the spirit that one apprehends the life of another. And such recognition gives courage in the assurance that one is on the right road, that God is with us both. If he is there, our failure shall come out his success.

WRITTEN ON A TRANS-PACIFIC STEAMER:

A violin is wailing its heartbreaking strains to the accompaniment of a piano. The strains come to me from below mingled with the sound of the sea that is like the sound of a steady wind moving in the top of a forest—man's heartbreak mingled with the meanings of the Infinite and in harmony with his purposes of love.

WHILE AT THE SEASHORE

I was out morning and night to see the high tides that roared as they plunged landward, bounding and retreating. A storm at sea made grandeur for us here. I have been bursting happy as I faced the great sea and its powerful, surging waves, and listened to the deep, deep roar coming from far out until it broke in a crash at my feet. No amount of rain could dampen my exalted spirits.

A flight of birds swept up from the plain—joyous wanderers of the air, circling near at hand. In a twinkling they vanish, like a picture washed from the slate. Where did they go? They went not. They are still there, skimming and flying, rising, falling, sailing, full of grace and exquisite charm. But you saw them against the background of sky. A mountain arose between the flight and the sky and its earthly hue absorbs the vision; but they are there still circling in the clear air, only the eye cannot discern them because the bright background of sky is changed for one of earth.

It is only ourselves who prevent the accomplishment of anything the Lord gives us to do. He is infinitely more interested than we in bringing about results. Therefore we need to merge our will in his.

In John 15. 7, we are taught how to realize large answers to our prayers. We must remember the twofold condition the Lord here lays down: we in him and his word in us. Love and Right. Let our personal wish be lost in his word of Truth, and our will be directed by personal love for him: then 'ye shall ask what ye will, and it shall be done unto you.'

The only danger is that one's will becomes weakened and his ideas warped by thinking too much without wholesome food for thought—thinking that becomes brooding. Thinking of one's temptation and weakness overmuch makes one an easier victim next time. If you wish to banish wrong thoughts, apply the mind to good thoughts. Let it run into a train of thoughts started by some author, or seek the company of someone who can help thought.

Learn to await God's time, to walk in his way. Be sure if, after you have looked to him, the way is thoroughly closed, he does not want you there, at least not then.

To young people amid careless life, happy life, times of unrest and aspiration, longings and yearnings unutterable stir within. Trust the stirring within. It is the voice of God. It is your title to heaven. You may not interpret into action just as God intends, but trust and go ahead. God will see that you go right. You may hear a voice saying, 'Come up higher, higher to the heights,' and you see looming before you magnificent heights, and it seems to you all glorious. You seek the way up and find that you only go down. A voice says, 'Come up.' Your footsteps seem forced downward. It seems as if the voice was of the imagination and that God mocks. Trust if for no other reason than because for you there is no other better than that same voice. Trust even though the way seems down. Trust and God will take you over only what will prove to be a valley between you and the real upward way—perhaps the valley of humiliation which skirts the mountains of God. Trust and you shall stand upon heights glorious with the glory of God, so high above your own interpretation of God's will and ways that your own interpretation has sunk out of sight in the prospect that spreads below, as the hills are hidden and are lost from the mountaintop.

It is a delicate thing to attempt to sketch the inner life of one so far removed from the average soul as hers. We can set our camera, but when we have finished the picture it is only a photogravure as unlike the radiant original as is the frontispiece of this book. We can paint the form and suggest the colour of the violet, but what brush can paint its fragrance? Her religious life even where it resembles others' was original—the product not of the stencil plate, but a free-hand drawing, having an incidence of light, a sentiment, a touch which no artist can exactly reproduce. Her religion, though having a form, was a life.

One of its elements was its strength. Her faith was more than a pious feeling; it was a conviction, deep rooted in doctrine, fact, and experience. While she had no patience with speculative discussions of truth that aimed at no practical end, she was herself fond of searching the inner depths of those great Bible doctrines for which the evangelical church stands. Many a time when our conversation led to these fundamentals of saving truths, we have been startled not only by the clearness of her apprehension of them but also by the way in which she massed the reasons for them. And they stood in her mind related, coordinated, a complete system.

This wealth of conviction was not wholly, or even chiefly, intellectual. She had a feminine intuition; her insight was keen and her outlook was clear. What she perceived to be true, her heart appropriated with absorbing love, and she at once sought to work it into practical life. The daily necessities of her earnest work in China made it impossible for her to confound clear thinking with the joy of truth, or to mistake pious feelings for the bloom of character. To her feeling was a force to impel to action—a force which would really weaken the soul unless it was spent in some useful work.

These were the features of her spiritual life that most impressed those who were associated with her in daily work—strength of conviction and an invincible energy in turning every force to practical ends. A friend once remarked to her that this was the secret of the vigorous healthful tone of her interior life, and her reply was deep with significance: "Just the reverse. It is the inner life that explains the outer." She had deep aspirations for the divine, and gave herself to earnest struggle for its attainment by prayer, meditation, and self-sacrifice. The "open reward" which we observed had its spring in the closet with the "closed door." Hers was a spirituality which under different conditions would have made her a mystic of the Fletcher or Madam Guyon type.

In the spring of 1894 she came into an experience which she declared was something more than the natural unfolding of her spiritual life. It was a crisis, radical and far reaching. It illuminated and vitalized all she had before, and put new significance into all that came after. She gave it no name, only it was manifested in her consciousness by a profound sense of the abiding presence of the personal Saviour. It was the raising of her affections to the height of a holy and self-renouncing enthusiasm, together with an absolute rest in the sovereign will of Him who enfolded her—her work and all things else besides—and a perfect relief from all sense of bondage in every service however laborious, exacting, costly, or self-denying it might be. She rarely spoke of this experience in any detail, knowing full well that it would not be understood. But in trying to help one very dear to her through a spiritual crisis she wrote the following letter:

> Let me tell you about something that has come to me. For years I have loved goodness because goodness is a lovely thing. I have tried to be good. Later on I more and more tried to let Christ make me good. Still later I came to know that all goodness is in Christ and that we can be good only in the degree that we let Christ live in us.
>
> As the years passed I began to forget myself some and to be more constantly concerned for others, for their own sakes and for Christ's sake. Lately I have felt that I would give my life to see accomplished my desires for certain ones dear to me. But my

prayers seemed thwarted. The opposite of my desires seemed to develop. I myself came to feel more and more helpless, as if I did not know what to pray for, how to live, what choices to make, or anything else. One day, consumed by a feeling of helplessness, knowing God is true and *right*, I succumbed before a sense of helpless misery. With no desire but to know and do his will and to be a help to others, I seemed only to mistake as to what his will was, and to hinder others.

Tired, undone, knowing Christ was near, but getting no comfort from the knowledge, I sat weighted and dully wondered how I should ever stand or go. My misery had begun in anxiety for others, turned to misery because my effort to help failed, and seemed to fail because of something wrong in me, and I could *not see* where the wrong was, and I was so tired it seemed as if I could not try any more. Slowly my eyes had been opening, and now I saw myself as I suppose the tender Father had seen me all the time.

The chilling, heavy clouds gathered closer. I sat inert, every possibility of resistance gone. The billows seemed to roll slowly over me and roll back again. Wave after wave, with no voice to cry, no prayer to offer. I sat still, I knew too much of Christ's and of God's love to let doubt enter to kill faith at this critical time. Somehow I seemed to feel that my misery was a part of God's working. So, beaten, undone, I was still, still before God— empty, entirely empty. If any human heart ever was empty, mine was then.

Then what a strong, soft brooding Presence enfolded me, lifted me steadily until I *rested*! Tired and just as undone as before, I yet felt his arms. Deep peace crept in strong waves through my being. 'As one whom his mother comforted' I rested, every care rolled off. I knew with deep assurance, '*All is well.*' Past and future he cares for, my burden gone, entirely taken by him. Gracious and full of power, I felt I *knew him*. It was the Lord! If you understand me, I dare say *I saw him*! Since then everything has been different. It is so *easy* to cast my care upon him.

There is a purpose in my telling you all this. I think there is help for *you* in it. *Ask God to help you* understand the meaning that my words may not make clear. . . . About serving God: *total* surrender is one condition. *Believe his Word.* It is for *you* to will that you will *trust* him. When you put yourself into his hands, and assert *no* will of your own as to what he shall do with you, then wait and trust; he will empty and fill again. He will show you by his spirit what to do and how to do it.

Much of this was hers during all the previous years of her religious life. Only the sense of the divine presence could have sustained that habitual cheerfulness and that triumphant hopefulness which characterized her in the depressing environment in which she toiled. Everyone associated with her there remarked the triumphant temper of her mind. She was an optimist both by nature and by grace. The most troublesome problems which often perplexed the Mission, never for a moment clouded her vision of the final outcome. She knew that the sovereign Will was holding its straight line through all these complexities. She saw the horses and chariots of God among the hills round about Dothan.

It was a faith quickened by the indwelling Spirit that explains her splendid hopefulness. She was ever broadminded, and studied events in their relation to the great world movements rather than from the centre of her own particular work. For this reason she was never overmuch depressed when her projects varied from the line she herself had planned. Their orbit, like those of the planets, varied from the perfect ellipse because they were a part of the universe order. For this reason also things which from a narrow and selfish view seemed meagre and purposeless acquired for her an unspeakable significance and grandeur because a part of that everlasting universe in which God is sovereign.

We are inclined to think that that experience of 1894 was the rapid and consummate bloom of a flower, every element of which had been pulsing in the plant from bulb to bud. And that splendid outburst meant the approach of the end. God spared her long enough for us to see what such a life as hers would produce—a sweet memory and a holy motive to similar consecration.

During the summer of 1906 symptoms of arterial hardening appeared, and by the advice of an eminent specialist, she was taken to a sanatorium for treatment. But as she did not improve, it was thought best for her to return to Summit, New Jersey, where she could be near her physician and have the loving ministries of her home. The arterial hardening, however, was rapid in its progress and attacked the cerebral vessels. While her mind was perfectly clear until a few weeks before the end, a form of aphasia occurred in which it was impossible for her readily to command words.

She was thus prevented during eight long weeks of confinement to the sick room from communicating by speech with those who loved her, and who would have prized words from her lips at such a time as gems of incalculable value. But they were not without communications from her, truer perhaps and with larger revelations of her soul, because not confined within the bounds of limiting speech. Her spirit seeking expression, beamed in her countenance with a luminosity that was not of this earth, a solar light such as no artist could possibly paint about the heads of his saints. There was a spiritual communion in that sick chamber, akin to that which a soul has with God, and as real.

By a happy providence there was granted another means, and one akin to that we have just mentioned, of learning her innermost mind as she approached the end of her earthly career. Mr. Gamewell had recently given her a new Bible in which she had marked such passages as specially appealed to her during her last months. Thus the Word of God was the spoken word of her soul to those who were dear to her. These marked passages indicated unmistakably that she anticipated the near approach of this significant hour, and that she was ready for it. They revealed her perfect confidence in her Saviour and her full assurance of victory. The following are selections, the italicized words indicating her own underlining.

"Study to shew thyself approved unto God" (2 Tim. 2. 15).

"Thou therefore endure hardness, as a good soldier of Jesus Christ" (2 Tim. 2. 3).

"*And whatsoever ye do in word or deed, do all in the name of the Lord Jesus*, giving thanks to God and the Father by him" (Col. 3. 17).

"*And whatsoever ye do, do* IT HEARTILY AS TO THE LORD, *and not unto men*; knowing that of the Lord ye shall receive the reward of the inheritance: *for ye serve the Lord Christ*" (Col. 3. 23, 24).

"But my God shall supply all your needs according to his riches in glory by Christ Jesus" (Phil. 4. 19).

"*For thou hast been a strength to the poor, a strength to the needy in his distress, a refuge from the storm, a shadow from the heat, when the blast from the terrible ones is as a storm against the wall*" (Isa. 25. 4).

"Because they *received not the* LOVE OF THE TRUTH, that they might be saved" (2 Thess. 2. 10).

"And the Lord direct your hearts into the love of God, and into *the patient waiting for Christ*" (2 Thess. 3. 5).

"Be ye also patient; stablish your hearts: for the coming of the Lord draweth nigh" (Jas. 5. 8).

"For ye have need of patience, that, after ye have done the will of God, ye might receive the promise" (Heb. 10. 36).

"And when the chief Shepherd shall appear, ye shall receive a crown of glory that fadeth not away" (1 Pet. 5. 4).

"And who is he that will harm you, if ye be followers of that which is good?" (1 Pet. 3. 13).

"For God hath not given us the spirit of fear; but of power, and of love, and of a sound mind" (2 Tim. 1. 7).

"For he looked for a city which hath foundations, whose builder and maker is God" (Heb. 11. 10).

"And so much the more as ye see the day approaching" (Heb. 10. 25).

"Casting all your care upon him; for he careth for you" (1 Pet. 5. 7).

"And this is the promise that he hath promised us, even eternal life" (1 John 2. 25).

"For I know whom I have believed, and am persuaded that he is able to keep that which I have committed unto him against that day" (2 Tim. 1. 12).

"And now, little children, *abide in him; that, when he shall appear, we may have confidence, and not be ashamed before him at his coming"* (1 John
2. 28).

"And this is life eternal, that they might know thee the only true God, and Jesus Christ, whom thou hast sent" (John 17. 3).

"It is a faithful saying: For if we be dead with him, we shall also live with him" (2 Tim. 2. 11).

"But as it is written, Eye hath not seen, nor ear heard, neither have entered into the heart of man, the things which God hath prepared for them that love him. *But God hath revealed them unto us by his Spirit"* (1 Cor. 2. 9, 10).

"And let the peace of God rule in your hearts, to the which also ye are called in one body; and be ye thankful" (Col. 3. 15).

"If ye then be risen with Christ, seek those things which are above, where Christ sitteth at the right hand of God. Set your affection on things above, not on things on the earth" (Col. 3. 1,1).

"He will swallow up death in victory; and the Lord God will wipe away

tears from off all faces" (Isa. 25. 8).

"And in that day ye shall ask me nothing" (John 16. 23).

"O death, where is thy sting? O grave, where is thy victory? The sting of death is sin; and the strength of sin is the law. But thanks be to God, which giveth us the victory through our Lord Jesus Christ" (1 Cor. 15. 55-57). On the margin of this passage Mrs. Gamewell penned: "In *life* as well as in death."

"Therefore, my beloved brethren, be ye steadfast, unmoveable, always abounding in the work of the Lord, forasmuch as ye know that your labour is not in vain in the Lord" (1 Cor. 15. 58).

Those who feel most keenly the sorrow of their bereavement are sure that her final appeal to them is, "Be ye steadfast, unmoveable, always abounding in the work of the Lord, forasmuch as ye know that your labour is not in vain in the Lord."

On November 17 her last audible word was spoken, and from that time she lingered either fully or partially unconscious till November 27, 1906, when her spirit took its flight.

She has left a precious memory, a character beautiful in its union of gentleness and strength, a life great in courage and in entire consecration to others' good, a religion which has its full expression in the words she loved so well, "All for Jesus." When we looked upon those still lips once so eloquent with the gospel message, it was borne in upon our hearts that this is a part of the immense price of China's redemption.

The funeral services were private, and were held in the parsonage of the Methodist Episcopal church in Summit, New Jersey, which had been her home for several years, and where she died. The services were conducted by Bishop E. G. Andrews and Bishop J. W. Bashford. We reverently bore the "sacred dust" to Fairmount Cemetery in Hackensack, New Jersey, where Mr. Gamewell's kindred are sepulchercd. Rev. G. M. Fowles read the service at the grave, and we returned to our work feeling that loyalty to her memory impelled us to a larger devotion than ever to the cause to which she had given her life. Already *the blood of the martyrs is the seed of the church.*

LEONAUR

ALSO FROM LEONAUR
AVAILABLE IN SOFTCOVER OR HARDCOVER WITH DUST JACKET

THE RELUCTANT REBEL by William G. Stevenson—A young Kentuckian's experiences in the Confederate Infantry & Cavalry during the American Civil War..

BOOTS AND SADDLES by Elizabeth B. Custer—The experiences of General Custer's Wife on the Western Plains.

FANNIE BEERS' CIVIL WAR by Fannie A. Beers—A Confederate Lady's Experiences of Nursing During the Campaigns & Battles of the American Civil War.

LADY SALE'S AFGHANISTAN by Florentia Sale—An Indomitable Victorian Lady's Account of the Retreat from Kabul During the First Afghan War.

THE TWO WARS OF MRS DUBERLY by Frances Isabella Duberly—An Intrepid Victorian Lady's Experience of the Crimea and Indian Mutiny.

THE REBELLIOUS DUCHESS by Paul F. S. Dermoncourt—The Adventures of the Duchess of Berri and Her Attempt to Overthrow French Monarchy.

LADIES OF WATERLOO by Charlotte A. Eaton, Magdalene de Lancey & Juana Smith—The Experiences of Three Women During the Campaign of 1815: Waterloo Days by Charlotte A. Eaton, A Week at Waterloo by Magdalene de Lancey & Juana's Story by Juana Smith.

TWO YEARS BEFORE THE MAST by Richard Henry Dana. Jr.—The account of one young man's experiences serving on board a sailing brig—the Penelope—bound for California, between the years 1834-36.

A SAILOR OF KING GEORGE by Frederick Hoffman—From Midshipman to Captain—Recollections of War at Sea in the Napoleonic Age 1793-1815.

LORDS OF THE SEA by A. T. Mahan—Great Captains of the Royal Navy During the Age of Sail.

COGGESHALL'S VOYAGES: VOLUME 1 by George Coggeshall—The Recollections of an American Schooner Captain.

COGGESHALL'S VOYAGES: VOLUME 2 by George Coggeshall—The Recollections of an American Schooner Captain.

TWILIGHT OF EMPIRE by Sir Thomas Ussher & Sir George Cockburn—Two accounts of Napoleon's Journeys in Exile to Elba and St. Helena: Narrative of Events by Sir Thomas Ussher & Napoleon's Last Voyage: Extract of a diary by Sir George Cockburn.

www.ingramcontent.com/pod-product-compliance
Lightning Source LLC
Chambersburg PA
CBHW032057080426
42733CB00006B/310